MANIPULATION TECHNIQUES

Discover How to Analyze People Through Mind Manipulation, Psychological Techniques and Body Language

Judith Dawson

© Copyright 2020 by Judith Dawson. All right reserved.

The work contained herein has been produced with the intent to provide relevant knowledge and information on the topic on the topic described in the title for entertainment purposes only. While the author has gone to every extent to furnish up to date and true information, no claims can be made as to its accuracy or validity as the author has made no claims to be an expert on this topic. Notwithstanding, the reader is asked to do their own research and consult any subject matter experts they deem necessary to ensure the quality and accuracy of the material presented herein.

This statement is legally binding as deemed by the Committee of Publishers Association and the American Bar Association for the territory of the United States. Other jurisdictions may apply their own legal statutes. Any reproduction, transmission or copying of this material contained in this work without the express written consent of the copyright holder shall be deemed as a copyright violation as per the current legislation in force on the date of publishing and subsequent time thereafter. All additional works derived from this material may be claimed by the holder of this copyright.

The data, depictions, events, descriptions and all other information forthwith are considered to be true, fair and accurate unless the work is expressly described as a work of fiction. Regardless of the nature of this work, the Publisher is exempt from any responsibility of actions taken by the reader in conjunction with this work. The Publisher acknowledges that the reader acts of their own accord and releases the author and Publisher of any responsibility for the observance of tips, advice, counsel, strategies and techniques that may be offered in this volume.

TABLE OF CONTENTS

Introduction 1
Chapter 1 *What Is Manipulation?* 4
Chapter 2 *The Subconscious Mind And The Key To Manipulation* 10
Chapter 3 *How To Use Manipulation* 13
Chapter 4 *Emotional Manipulation* 23
Chapter 5 *Mind Control* 27
Chapter 6 *Neuro-Linguistic Programming* 32
Chapter 7 *Body Language* 39
Chapter 8 *Persuasion* 42
Chapter 9 *Hypnosis* 48
Chapter 10 *Reverse Psychology* 52
Chapter 11 *Brainwashing* 55
Chapter 12 *Seduction* 58
Chapter 13 *Spotting Manipulation* 64
Conclusion 68
Description 70

INTRODUCTION

Manipulation—it is something that everyone thinks they have an opinion on, but no one quite realizes what the truth of the matter is. Is it good? Bad? Always negative? Can it be used positively sometimes? All of these are hard to answer for most people—it becomes difficult to understand where the lines can be drawn. The truth is, like with just about anything else out there, the truth to manipulation is that it can be good *or* bad. It can be used to influence people to help them become better, or it can be used to destroy someone's very sense of being.

Manipulation is used widely throughout the world. We use it when we negotiate and haggle, believe it or not. We use it when we attempt to persuade someone else to do something. Even the most honest salespeople out there are manipulating you in their own ways—and this is just fine. It is okay that they are doing so—it is okay that they have their own ways to do what they do. It doesn't necessarily make them good or bad—it just means that they are using manipulation.

Ultimately, the word manipulate refers to the act of molding something else. You manipulate clay; for example—you use your hands to change the shape. The word itself comes from French, which drew from Latin's *manipulus,* meaning handful. This is precisely what manipulation is as well—it is a sense of molding someone else into what you want them to be. Now, whether that manipulation is innocent or not depends primarily on what follows after the fact. Do you manipulate in hopes of getting your way when you are trying to do something? Do you do so in hopes of bettering the other person? The intention behind the manipulation matters—and that intention can vary greatly from person to person. Depending upon how you choose to utilize it, your own manipulation of other people can vary immensely. You just have to figure out what you will do with it when you do spot it.

Imagine a situation in which Alice tells Bob that she really likes his steak so much better than her own. She really loves how, when he cooks it, the salt crystallizes just right, and there is a beautiful sear on all sides. Alice raves and raves about the steak that Bob makes—and Bob then decides to make some steak for the two of them. Is this manipulation? Technically, it is—it is actively attempting to alter the way in which someone else is behaving. You are intentionally trying to make it a point to take over the situation that you are in. You are forcing your own personal point through attempting to influence the way that the people around you see the world.

It is technically manipulative, but is that as harmful as someone who may be attempting to groom someone else into being a lifelong victim? Probably not—we have all sorts of different manipulative situations in which sometimes, people choose to engage with people in ways that are not actually helpful. We have these situations in which sometimes, people are controlled for nefarious or selfish purposes, and we also have situations in which we are influenced for other reasons. A doctor may employ manipulation to gain compliance with medical treatment; for example—they may insist that, if the patient does not comply, they are likely to die long before their children come of age, for example. Technically, this is manipulative, as we will be addressing shortly. Just because something is manipulative is not inherently problematic- the problem comes with the intent that follows. If you choose to manipulate other people, you can do so without much of a problem, even ethically, if done for the right reason.

This book is here to begin to delve into the idea of manipulation of other people. Though traditionally wielded by people with darker, more sinister mindsets who only wanted to use and abuse people to get ahead, you are able to make use of many of these techniques in day-to-day situations in which you will be able to get the most out of them. You will be able to see that ultimately, you are able to do better with those that you engage in. You will be able to begin working on how you are able to better influence those around you in hopes that you will be able to make a real difference. We will be taking a look at several different examples of manipulation to begin to understand how it can be used and why that matters. We will spend the time to consider what manipulation is, how it works, and who cares to use it. We will be taking the time to look at all sorts of other information as well, such as what to expect with forms of manipulation. From emotional manipulation to persuasion and form NLP to taking a look at brainwashing and hypnosis. We will be exploring several different options, all of which have been used to some degree or another to control people around you. You may not feel like you are very susceptible, but the truth is, the human mind is surprisingly fragile. The human mind is surprisingly easy to influence and alter, and because of that, unsuspecting people can be highly influenced by ease if someone knows what they are doing.

Now, if you are not the kind to care to manipulate others, that's fine too— you can take a look at how you can begin to recognize these different tactics for what they are. As you continue to learn about the information that you will be reading within this book, you can begin to understand what is used to manipulate other people. You will be able to recognize what it will take to begin to control those around you, or you can choose to take that information with you to begin recognizing when others attempt to control you instead. Through this information, you should be able to understand what it will take to combat manipulation on yourself, or you can choose to utilize it to your advantage.

Keep in mind that manipulation is not always bad—you are able to persuade someone to take a look at purchasing an item that you identify as being the right one for them, even if they disagree at first. You are able to learn to negotiate like a champ with ease as well—learning to negotiate is something that typically involves body language, persuasion, and a bit of NLP sprinkled in for good measure. When you learn to use these methods and put them together, you are able to create a powerful force that people would be hard-pressed to challenge. When you continue to negotiate against other people, you are able to begin to take charge.

As you read through this book, make sure to keep an open mind. Some of the information might seem far-fetched at times—you might not think that you actually do have the control that you have over people, for example. Or, you might find that you are uncomfortable with the information that was presented to you. However, this information is good to have. If you do not know how to protect yourself, then you are going to struggle to spot the people that are the most likely to cause harm to you. With effort and some practice, you will be able to begin spotting what it is that you ought to be looking for. If you are able to do this for yourself, you will see that you are able to ultimately succeed.

Now, let's get started at diving into the world of manipulation. Hang on—it's going to be a wild ride.

CHAPTER 1
What Is Manipulation?

Manipulation itself is something that a lot of people fail to properly identify and label. It is something that is meant to be relatively easy to understand—it is as simple as influencing the reactions that someone else has, controlling the perspective that they have over what they are doing at any point in time. If you are able to recognize the influence that you have over those around you, you are able to begin to control how you engage with the world. You are able to begin to have better control over yourself as well, and that is highly powerful. If you want to be able to control how those that are in your vicinity behave, then you are in the right spot.

Within this chapter, we have a few primary objectives. We will set out how to define manipulation. We will be taking a look at how to begin identifying the ethics that go into manipulation, as well as how to understand who it is that manipulates other people. Finally, we will take a look at why people manipulate in the first place. This chapter will serve to set the foundation for everything else—you will be able to see precisely why so much of what is out there in this book is as sinister as it is just by seeing the people that the manipulation is based upon. As you read through the chapter, you should end with a better appreciation for what manipulation is and how important it can be.

Defining Manipulation

Psychological manipulation is a form of social influence that is designed to allow for the changing of the behaviors or the perceptions of other people through your own actions. Typically, the manipulative actions are indirect, deceptive, and sometimes even underhanded to get what is desired. Usually, as well, the entire purpose is to advance the interests of the individual interested in manipulating in the first place. It typically comes at the expense of someone else, but the manipulator typically does not care.

Social influence itself is not always a negative thing—it is something that allows for social pressures to mold us into what we ought to be at any point in time. If you want to make sure that you are working with yourself to better who you are, you will want to engage with your own social influences to help yourself begin that change. Doctors and nurses, for example, will influence our behaviors that directly influence our health and wellbeing. Family and friends might urge us to change up how we engage with other people. The social influence that we have is generally perceived as harmless within certain circles—it can be rejected or accepted and typically is not very coercive. However, manipulation usually goes a step further with the coercion that exists.

Is Manipulation Always Bad?
Of course, this begs the question of whether manipulation is something that is always, without fail, bad. The truth is, it is not. It is something that is actually surprisingly flexible. Manipulation itself is more akin to a tool than anything else. While it tends to be deceptive or underhanded, sometimes, that can be justified if the ends are the right ones. If you are able to get through a situation and get that proper end result, you know that what you are doing is going to be worth it. Certain situations simply make sense for manipulation to occur, such as in that example of a doctor or a nurse attempting to influence the treatment that someone gets. With this idea in mind, it becomes important to take a look at how you are able to define your own boundaries. How far do you want to go? What are you willing to do—and what are you not willing to accept? This information will help you. However, remember that manipulation itself is no worse than a gun or a knife. Used in the right context, both can be the difference between life and death—sometimes, you need a gun or a knife for protection, for hunting, or for general survival. Sometimes, they are just nice to have on hand for something. And, sometimes, they are used for nefarious purposes that would not help anyone.

Recognizing that manipulation is very similar in the sense that it cannot really be good or bad, but it can be accepted or rejected, you begin to see that ultimately, it is something of a tool. It really is just a tool that you are able to use to influence the minds of those around you, and if you get good at using this particular tool, you are able to find that your own skills and abilities are made dramatically better with ease.

Who Manipulates Others?
Manipulative people, especially those who are maliciously manipulative, have mastered the art of deceiving everyone around them. They have become highly skilled at being able to change who they are, how they engage with the world around them, and what they do at any point in time. They might seem to be perfectly nice from the outside, but oftentimes, this is entirely fake. They are there to draw their victims in. They want to make it clear to their targets that they are someone that should be trusted. After all, trust is one of the primary components to being able to manipulate someone unless you intend to resort to the blackmail of some sort.

Manipulative people are those who are not really interested in you unless you serve a purpose. They are there to gain control over people—they want to get their way as much as possible, and so long as you comply, they will allow you to continue on as if everything is relatively normal. However, if you don't comply, they tend to snap. They play the victim, or they lash out. Again, remember that at this point in time, we are primarily discussing the manipulators that are likely to be malicious in intent over all others.

Typically, the malicious manipulator lacks insight into how they engage with others, or they believe that the way that they have chosen to approach a situation is the right way that will meet their own needs above all others. They may be controllers or abusers. They do not care so much about what other people need—they want their own needs met. Boundaries? They have no regard for them! You tell them to keep their distance or to do something differently? They will pretend that they have not heard them, or they will simply completely override them, period. They will crowd you and push you about, willing to take control of the situation and you by all means—even if that means intimidation in hopes of getting you to comply.

They also tend to avoid their accountability—the skilled manipulator is never at fault, and they will always find a way to blame everyone else for the problems that they face. They see nothing wrong with refusing to take responsibility, but they will absolutely hold other people accountable as much as possible. They may even try to make their own problems yours as well in hopes of shirking off the responsibilities as simply as possible.

Typically, the most manipulative of all fall into what is known as the Dark Triad—they suffer from three dark traits that make them highly dangerous and ruthless. They do not care about hurting others because they have little regard for empathy or maintaining relationships. The Dark Triad consists of:

1. **The Narcissist:** The narcissist is someone suffering from narcissistic personality disorder. This person oftentimes finds themselves being incapable of empathy, struggling to see the world realistically, and will work to make themselves the center of attention at all costs. They work to make sure that they get the world that they want above all others and that world places them solely in the limelight. To the narcissist, no one can be better at anything than they are—otherwise, there is some egregious harm that must be dealt with.

2. **The Machiavellian:** The Machiavellian is someone who believes that the ends will always justify the means. To them, people are little more than tools to help them arrive at their final destination. They don't care so much about ensuring that they are well-liked—they just want to make sure that they get whatever it was that they were seeking, no matter what the cost may be. They will work as hard as they can to make sure that they get what they want, and they do not care how many people they have to step on to get there.

3. **The Psychopath:** Finally, the last person to consider is the psychopath. This is someone who simply does not care about other people. They do not care what it will take to get them what they want, and they will use people just because they can. These people lack any sense of empathy and do not seem to have any qualms with hurting those around them if it means that they will get whatever it is that they are looking for.

Ultimately, this dark triad becomes important to understand—most of the study of dark psychology, which the contents of this book heavily overlap with, will take a look through the eyes of these people with the Dark Triad. They tend to take what those on the Dark Triad would do and use that as a sort of emulation for how to get through everything. When you take a look at how these people tend to engage with each other and with those around them, you see that these people are dangerous, and they don't care what it takes to get what they were looking for in the first place.

Why Do People Manipulate?

Ultimately, people manipulate for all sorts of reasons. Some of the reasons are simply because of the fact that they fall into the Dark Triad. Others are forced into it. Others still have all sorts of reasons that they may choose to turn to manipulation for themselves and those around them. It is often that there are these very real reasons behind it, and when you begin to understand what they are, you realize the truth—that the manipulators that are out there are highly powerful.

Now, let's take a look at those common motivations for manipulators—understanding them would help you immensely with becoming capable of identifying those that may be manipulating you or those around you.

- **They have a need to push their own agendas:** Oftentimes, manipulators do so because they do not care about what happens to other people—but they do care about what happens to themselves. They find that they have something that they need to push, usually advancing their own personal gain, and they are willing to do so, even at a cost to those around them. They do not care—they just want to get what they want without having to deal with the waiting.
- **They have a strong need for superiority:** Often, you are able to see that manipulative individuals do engage in manipulation because they want to make themselves feel powerful. They want to make sure that ultimately, they are the ones that get to deal with what they do. They want to

make sure that those around them recognize that they are the superior ones, and they will push at all costs to make it happen for them. They will not hold back.
- **A need for control:** Sometimes, the motivator for the manipulator is simply getting control over a situation. Being in control of who those around them are is a great way to make sure that they are able to stay on top and that control is earned through learning to influence and manipulate others.
- **A need to feel power over others to boost self-esteem:** Sometimes, what is desired is a boost in self-esteem. When someone's self-esteem is lacking, it can be hard for them to really feel like they matter in the world. For some people, they make themselves feel more powerful and boost their self-esteem by making it a point to control others. They see that they have that control over someone else and that boosts how they feel. After all, it is difficult to be able to control others—they have to trust or hold you in a high enough regard to allow you to control them, and that allows for a bit of an ego boost as a result.
- **Boredom:** Sometimes, people are just bored. They want something that they can do to help themselves boost their own personal entertainment, and they choose to play a game. They are not really trying to hurt anyone or get ahead—they just want to play a game to alleviate that boredom and grant them the entertainment that they are looking for.
- **Covert agenda:** Sometimes, there is a genuine covert agenda underlying everything. This is a theory that not everyone is willing to accept—but it is there. Oftentimes, people see the world around them as a barrier to complete a covert agenda. Sometimes, for example, elderly people are targeted for the covert agenda of scamming them out of money because they are usually not as technologically savvy, and they also struggle to really understand everything else that goes into scams these days. When they get a phone call from their granddaughter, crying that she just got arrested a few states away for something silly and that she needs money ASAP, they tend to be swayed just by virtue of the fact that they care about their children or grandchildren. That is a covert agenda to steal the funds from elderly

individuals because they are deemed less likely to notice in the first place.
- **An inability to feel emotions:** Sometimes, the individual who manipulates others simply does not realize that they are doing so. They may struggle to, for example, feel their emotions or make sure that they can do better. They feel nothing that would usually hold people back from manipulating those around them, and without those underlying emotions, they do not really realize that they are manipulating in the first place. Or, they may find that they are so busy trying to convince themselves that their own emotions are false that they wind up hurting others instead.
- **Lacking self-control:** Some people are simply impulsive—they wind up being terrible at being able to control themselves and any of the urges that they have. With those impulses in place and no empathy to help them to hold back, these people wind up reacting in ways that become manipulative to others.

Of course, there can be other reasons to want to manipulate someone else as well. However, those are the most common and are the ones that you are the most likely to find yourself encountering as you go off on your own journey.

CHAPTER 2
The Subconscious Mind And The Key To Manipulation

Did you know that you are not actually aware of everything at all times? Even when it feels like you are, the truth is, there is a whole wide world out there, all of which is there to be explored and enjoyed. However, you are only enjoying those moments when your conscious mind states that you are, or if your unconscious mind decides that it will be a good time.

The truth is, the subconscious can be a bit tricky- it is that inner voice in the back of your head when you think. It is there to help you guide yourself or to make sure that ultimately, you do choose out the right situations. Your subconscious mind acts as a sort of automated feature in your mind—it allows you to work quickly and without as much regard to what you are doing at any point in time.

Think about it this way—your subconscious is your autopilot. We all do things throughout the day that eventually become so habitual that it would be more of a detriment to have to think about every single action as we do them. The most common way to think about this is by driving. By learning how to drive, you have to do everything consciously at first. New drivers are terrified of getting into an accident because they still must work on how they move, what they do, and the way that they will put their feet on the pedals. Over time, however, the more that they do this, they commit the act of driving to their subconscious minds. This is why people can drive while talking after they have gotten the hang of things. They realize that they are fully capable of getting through what they do, and they embrace it. When they drive, they can do so effectively—all because their unconscious minds take care of it for them.

The subconscious mind has weaknesses; however—it is surprisingly easy to take advantage of, and we will be exploring this idea shortly. When it comes to the subconscious mind, you must be aware of this easily exploited weakness because if you do not take steps to avoid the problem, then you are far more likely to run into issues.

The Subconscious Mind

When it comes to the mind, the subconscious plays a few key roles. The subconscious is responsible for keeping you safe and alive. It is there to navigate the world without requiring your awareness. Unfortunately, the human mind is only able to focus and actually comprehend one thing at a time in any effective capacity. This means that, while you are reading, you are not really absorbing, consciously speaking, whatever is going on around you. You might be reading this book, and there could be people right behind you, having a conversation. You probably do not really catch the gist of what is being said. However, if something that they say doesn't sound quite right, or it is something that is directly about you or something relevant to you, you suddenly realize that you were paying attention all along. That's thanks to your subconscious mind.

Your senses are always working. They're constantly attempting to perceive what is happening around you. Even though you may not be consciously processing what the people around you are saying, you are still subconsciously recording it. Your subconscious mind then determines how to respond. If it is something important, it gets bumped up to your conscious mind. If it is not, then it is left to fall behind. This is imperative to note—when you pay attention to this, you start to realize that, ultimately, the way that your mind works is ingenious. You have the conscious part where you are able to focus, and your subconscious works as a sort of backup—it pays just enough attention to your surroundings to actively turn your attention there if necessary. This allows you to not have to waste conscious effort on everything you do—rather, you are able to only pay attention to what is pertinent at the moment.

Of course, this means that your subconscious is also out of your current awareness. You are not aware of it consciously because your conscious mind can only focus on one thing at a time. As you will see with many of the different options that we will be discussing, manipulation itself can happen within the subconscious mind in several different manners, all because you are unaware of your subconscious.

Manipulating the Subconscious Mind

When it comes to manipulation, then you are primarily targeting the subconscious. This is because your subconscious mind is what will pick up on your attempts to manipulate. The subconscious mind becomes capable of perceiving everything, but it also does not filter. Your conscious mind is not aware of what the subconscious perceives, and because of that, manipulation can occur easily. This is precisely how manipulation in the form of altering body language works—when you alter your own body language to attempt to influence or control the other person, you also create a situation in which you are being perceived by the subconscious mind of someone else. That subconscious then alters the way that you behave.

Think about the last time that you did something without thinking about it. Perhaps you found yourself standing in the same position as those around you. Maybe you found yourself feeling small without really understanding why. This is due to the fact that you are ruled by the way that your body moves. You are controlled by the way that you tend to behave solely because of your subconscious mind. Because it is your subconscious mind's job to keep you safe and alive, it is constantly filtering out how you behave. It is always influencing how you approach situations and what you do. This is its downfall, however, and as you continue to read on, you will see why.

The reason behind the fact that the subconscious is so easily influenced is because your subconscious is responsible for emotions. This is why your emotions that you have will never fully be within your control. No matter how hard you may try, there is no way that you are able to tell yourself, "Yes, I am happy now," or "No, I'm miserable or angry or frustrated." You cannot simply persuade yourself to feel a certain way— you feel what you feel, and that's that. However, the reason behind this is because your subconscious creates those feelings that you have.

This is powerful for one specific reason—your feelings create actions. There is a cycle that is commonly accepted within psychology, particularly in cognitive psychology, in which your thoughts, feelings, and behaviors are all intricately linked together. Your thoughts influence your feelings. Your feelings influence your behaviors. As a result, your behaviors also have a role in reinforcing those unconscious thoughts that you had. This all works together to create that cycle. Manipulation works by changing up one of the three rungs in the cycle—it works by causing some sort of shift in thoughts, feelings, or behaviors, which then changes the rest of the cycle as well.

Most commonly, manipulators will attack either thoughts or feelings— both of those are the easiest points of contact to control the other person. It is simple to make someone think a certain way if you know what you are doing, and this will be a primary focus when we take a look at neuro-linguistic programming. Alternatively, controlling emotions also comes easily if you know what you are doing—it just takes you being able to control yourself well enough to actually get the effect that you are looking for. For example, you might alter someone's emotions by controlling how you talk to them or how you present yourself. One way that we will discuss in persuasion involves appealing to the emotions of other people. Ultimately, through making it a point to influence the emotions of others, you then trigger their behaviors to be different as well.

Manipulators are experts at this. They are skilled at finding the weak point in figuring out what needs to be done. When you look at this with the idea of hijacking one's thoughts, feelings, and behaviors, you realize that ultimately, that power is there. You realize that the power that manipulation has runs far deeper than you probably thought possible. As you read through this book, you will begin to see it all play out—you will learn about how these interactions work for you and how you are able to use them in your own favor.

CHAPTER 3
How To Use Manipulation

When it comes to being able to use manipulation, there are a few different factors to consider. If you want to manipulate someone else, you must meet three primary criteria that all must come into play. You must be willing to conceal your own aggressive intentions, as well as be well aware of the vulnerabilities of your target. Finally, you must also be ruthless. All of this comes together to create the effect of manipulation that you are looking for in these situations. When you are able to make use of manipulation, you usually will follow through with certain methods of control, and there are usually very specific vulnerabilities as well.

Within this chapter, we will be addressing this idea of how to use manipulation, as well as what it will take to control people. We are going to be focused on several of the most common methods of control, along with the most common vulnerabilities that are targeted to exploit. When it comes to being able to control other people, it takes effort and an understanding of the underlying information as well. If you know what you are doing, however, you will be able to thrive at controlling the situations that you are in, no matter what kind of situation that may be.

Conceal Aggressive Intentions

First, you must make sure that your aggressive intentions are hidden. Typically, manipulation is considered aggressive because of the fact that it is usually attempting to control other people. This, in and of itself, is aggressive and must be managed well. If you want to be able to manipulate other people, one of the best ways of doing so is by making it a point to remain hidden. This is because most of the time, manipulation only works when the other party is unsuspecting.

Think about it—if you know that someone is intentionally trying to manipulate you, are you going to want to do what they wanted? Probably not—you will probably try to do anything in your power to prevent a repeat of what is happening. However, if you do not know that the other person is acting in a calculated manner to try to maintain control over you, you aren't going to go out of your way to stop it. This is why being able to control through the subconscious is so important—when you work to control someone from their subconscious mind instead of from their conscious mind, you are able to get further just by virtue of the fact that you are working to remain hidden.

Know Vulnerabilities

Additionally, it becomes imperative to understand and recognize the fact that the manipulator, in order to be effective, will need to have a solid understanding of the vulnerabilities of their target. They must make it a point to understand which of the psychological vulnerabilities will get them the best possible result and how they can go about it. When it comes to being able to spot those vulnerabilities, you realize that ultimately, you are able to begin to figure out how to control other people. Imagine that you know that someone is vulnerable to being left to feel like they are worthless. If you know that when they feel worthless, they start to wonder how they can make themselves do better and therefore feel better as well. When you consider the idea of being able to encourage people to feel in very specific manners, you will then be able to take advantage of them if you choose to do so. If you want to be able to control people around you, you must first begin to figure out how to chip down the defenses of the other person. You have to work toward bringing down those walls that surround people, so you are able to create your own network. You do this, so you are able to make sure that you will be working with strings that are powerful. In doing this in this manner, you show yourself how you are able to get control of a situation.

Be Ruthless

Finally, if you want to be able to use manipulation, you must be ruthless. You can't let your own guilt eat at you for being dishonest or for doing something for yourself. The best manipulators are those that are unafraid. They are the ones that are willing to do just about anything if they want to be able to get what they want. They are the people who have no problems being willing to do what it will take to succeed. This ruthlessness doesn't have to mean that you are cruel or evil—it just means that you are willing to do whatever it takes to make sure that you get your way. It means that you do not have to feel bad for what you do—you just have to do it.

This can be something that many people grapple with if they want to learn to get that control over people as well. However, it is something they will have to do if they want to succeed. If they want to be able to succeed at manipulating people or controlling people, they will need to be able to actually have that ruthlessness that will allow them to do so without feeling so bad about it.

Methods of Control

Ultimately, when it comes to controlling people, there are several different methods that work well. All of these methods of control are fantastic ways for manipulators to control their victims. As we go through these different methods of control, think about them—these will be relevant as we go through the future chapters as you begin to discover what it is that you will do to influence others.

Positive reinforcement

First, there is the usage of positive reinforcement. To use positive reinforcement is to attempt to convince the other person to continue to do something by rewarding the behavior. Positive reinforcement is what you get when a desirable event or stimulus is presented after a behavior

in hopes of getting that behavior to continue again in the future. Think about the idea of training your puppy by providing them with a treat every time they obey you or do something that you want them to do. By rewarding the behavior with positive reinforcement, they see that they get something that they want when they do what you want. There are all sorts of different ways that this can play out, such as with someone who chooses to love to bomb their partner in hopes of making them want to continue doing what they want. Positive reinforcement usually includes methods such as:
- Apologies
- Approval
- Attention
- Expressions
- Gifts
- Money
- Praise
- Recognition
- Superficial charm
- Superficial sympathy

Negative reinforcement
Negative reinforcement refers to the idea of removing a negative situation as a reward for behaviors. You are taking away something unpleasant when you see the other person do something that they should have. For example, if you were to ground your child for not cleaning his room, negative reinforcement would be allowing your child to then leave the room upon completing the task. You are putting your child under pressure in hopes that they will be willing and able to do what it will take to get them back on track to doing what they need to do. Negative reinforcement usually involves you creating an unpleasant situation in the first place, though this is not always a requirement.

Intermittent reinforcement
Intermittent reinforcement is one of the strongest because it creates doubt and fear. When you utilize this particular form of reinforcement, you run into other problems—you run into a situation in which you find that being hot and cold actually makes you seem more attractive to the other person. The idea is that because you are pleasant to be around sometimes, the individual will seek you out, and will double down and persist when you are not. This is the same sort of logic that has led to gambling addictions—it is the idea that you are able to get what you want if you know what you are doing, and that is highly powerful. If you want to be able to control the situation around you, the best thing that you are able to do is make it a point to make yourself unpredictable.

Punishment

Punishment is the intentional reaction toward someone to discourage behavior through negative events. It happens when you intentionally inflict discomfort or pain onto someone else in hopes of being able to control them better. You want them to feel like what they have done is unacceptable or is something that ought not to have happened, so you make it a point to take things out on them. Punishment typically can be just about anything, but some of the most common forms include:
- Crying
- Emotional blackmail
- Guilt trip
- Intimidation
- Nagging
- Playing the victim
- Silent treatment
- Sulking
- Swearing
- Threats
- Yelling

Traumatic one-trial learning
Finally, when you use traumatic one-trial learning, you are making it a point to use explosive anger, abuse, or attempts to establish dominance over a situation. It could be verbal and emotional, or it could be physical. When it comes to being able to utilize this, the victim is conditioned or trained rapidly to walk on eggshells around the manipulator for fear of exposing the problems. The victim does not want to end up in a situation in which they trigger the anger because they know what will come next—they know that ultimately, they will find themselves hurt or upset if they dare to frustrate their manipulator. They obey out of fear, and this allows for compliance to be held rather simply.

Common Manipulative Techniques

When it comes to the most common techniques that exist, most manipulation tactics fall into one of several simple categories. These different techniques are incredibly effective over time—they are able to keep people down, so the manipulator is able to do what he or she wants. If you learn to understand these different methods, you will start to recognize the patterns—you will see that ultimately, you are able to control people, or your eyes will be opened to the truth, so you are able to protect yourself as well. Let's go over some of those most common forms of manipulation now:
- **Bandwagon effect:** In using this method to manipulate, manipulators make it a point to gain submission by pointing out how everyone else uses these items or that everyone else similar to them does something. It is meant to feed on peer

pressure to make sure that the individual wants to move forward with something. This is commonly used to try to influence an individual to do something that they may not have wanted to do in the first place.
- **Brandishing anger:** When manipulators make use of their anger, they use it to attempt to keep their victims intimidated so that they can continue to maintain control over the situation. They want to shock the victim into being submissive again, and the manipulator will do this primarily through attempting to appear angry, even though they may not actually be frustrated at all—they just want the benefits from the anger. They often use this as a manipulation tactic to make sure that those around them are kept back. It helps them to avoid confrontation and allows them to continue to hide the truth because the victim will be too startled and, therefore, too timid to do anything about it.
- **Covert intimidation:** When using this, the manipulator will put the victim on the defensive because they will use threats to try to keep them down. This is because, when the victim is on the defensive, they have no choice but to try to defend themselves, and that means that the attacks on the individual also come to a screeching halt.
- **Denial:** During denial, the manipulator entirely refuses to admit to something. They either try to obscure the truth, or they have other methods that they use to make sure that the truth does not come out. As a result, they are able to retain their own element of control over the situation.
- **Diversion:** In this instance, the manipulator refuses to give a straight answer to a question and instead attempts to get around it. The manipulator will most commonly attempt to redirect toward a completely different topic entirely.
- **Evasion:** This is similar to diversion, but in this case, there are often vague responses given, or the responses are irrelevant or rambling. The goal is to distract instead of diverting.
- **Feigning innocence or confusion:** The manipulator will sometimes simply play dumb—they refuse to be acknowledged as the problem entirely. They would much rather make it clear that they are not the true problem—they want to deny that they knew that there was a problem there

in the first place, and through doing this, they are able to maintain their semblance of innocence that they wanted.
- **Guilt-tripping:** When using guilt trips, the manipulator wants to convince the victim that they are selfish or that the victim is not actually deserving of what they have. This is done to make the victim feel guilty for gaining compliance.
- **Lying by omission:** This form of lying occurs when a significant amount of the actual truth of the matter is hidden away or obscured for some reason. This form of lying hopes to leave out detail without offering it up—though the lie never actually took place, they also made it a point to avoid offering up that information when they should have. When questioned, they most often object, saying that they weren't asked to tell anyone anything, and because of that, they are not at fault.
- **Lying:** It is hard to tell when someone else is lying if you do not know what to look for, and though the truth may come out eventually, it usually does so when it is too late to get anything done about it. One way to start cutting down the chances of being lied to is to make sure that you understand what to look for-- learning the body language, becoming more stringent with yourself, and working to find a way to prevent yourself from being a problem are all great ways to make sure that you are not being lied to.
- **Minimization:** This particular behavior is denial, with a side of rationalization. When using this, the manipulation claims that their behaviors are not harmful because they were not actually serious. This is most commonly seen with telling people that something that was taken seriously is actually just a joke and that the people should not be as offended about it.
- **Playing the servant:** When the manipulator does this, they act as if what they are doing is hidden under the guise of just doing their jobs. They say that they are obedient or they are serving someone else—they cloak their own agenda in their service in an attempt to obscure what they are doing.
- **Playing the victim:** In this case, the manipulator attempts to revert things so that the victim is actually the attacker, while the manipulator is the one that has suffered. This is done to get the manipulator that pity and sympathy that they were looking for.

- **Projecting the blame:** When manipulators realize that they are going to be caught, they very quickly project the blame onto other people. Most often, they will attempt to make the victim appear to have done something wrong and make it so that the victim is the one that gets blamed. They will also claim that they were the ones wronged to further disguise themselves. This kind of thinking is meant to make sure that the victim is kept down. The most common way of doing this is to accuse the victims of being deserving of the abuse or paint the victim as the true abuser in a situation.
- **Rationalization:** When it comes to rationalizing something, the manipulator is attempting to make excuses for behaviors that are flawed to some degree. They may, for example, attempt to explain away an action that raised red flags as being culture, or they may try to make you feel like you are the crazy one for questioning something.
- **Seduction:** When a manipulator uses seduction, they use charm, flattery, praise, and their own support in hopes of getting a victim to lower their defenses. In doing so, they are able to gain that loyalty that they were looking for, which allows for further control over the situation.
- **Selective inattention:** In this instance, the manipulator is attempting to avoid giving attention to something that may not support their cause or claim. By falling for this, you see that there are very real problems—the manipulator denies the problem by claiming that they were entirely unaware of the problem in the first place.
- **Shaming:** Some manipulators prefer the use of sarcasm and offensive comments in tandem to create doubt and fear in the individual to allow for further control. The manipulators in the world prefer this tactic because shame can be triggered with anything from a glance at each other to actually saying things that are meant to keep the victim down and afraid. Manipulators typically will use this to keep their victims from ever actually crossing them to make sure that they maintain that control they are looking for.
- **Vilifying the victim:** In this tactic, the victim is put on the defensive while also making it a point to hide the aggression behind what the manipulator is doing. At the same time, the manipulator makes it sound like the victim is the one

causing problems—the victim is painted as the true manipulator or abuser in this situation.

Common Vulnerabilities

Ultimately, there are several vulnerabilities that you must consider when it comes to dealing with manipulators. These are the easiest points in which someone can manipulate someone. If you are looking for a target, this list would be your starting list of figuring out who can be controlled, how they can be controlled, and why it matters. Consider all of these different exploitable vulnerabilities yourself:

- **The need to please:** This is the desire that some people have to make sure that everyone around them is getting what they want or need. It is that feeling that they must make sure that everyone is happy and that the happiness of others falls on their own shoulders.
- **Addiction to approval from others:** Some people find themselves entirely caught up in whether or not they can get approval from others that they are looking for. They find that they are entirely stuck needing to get that approval from others, and they will do anything in their power to make that happen.
- **A lack of assertiveness:** Some people simply cannot bring themselves to say no. They may try—but their own inability only brings them down. They find themselves stuck, unable to find a way to communicate their disagreement without feeling like they are vocalizing disapproval in a way that they should not have been.
- **Blurry sense of identity:** Some people simply do not have any real sense of who they are. They struggle with the idea that they can create either their own identities and that they have that power over themselves, and as a result, they are easy to take advantage of. All the individuals have to do is push that sense of identity further and further until it can be taken advantage of as a result.
- **Low self-esteem:** Another major problem that leaves people vulnerable to abuse and manipulation is the lack of self-esteem. When you lack self-esteem, you find yourself in a position where you do not trust yourself. You would rather trust just about anyone else over yourself because you assume that they will be in the right. You assume that they will be far more likely to know what they are doing, and as such, you trust them over yourself.

- **Emetophobia:** This is the fear of emotions—particularly those that are negative. It is a fear of either expressing negative emotions or of being on the receiving end of negative emotions. When you fear the emotions of yourself and of those around you, you are able to run into significant problems that must be addressed. This can really hold you back if you do not know what you are able to do to begin to mitigate it.
- **Naivete:** When the victim is too naïve to realize that they are being taken advantage of, they make very easy targets that can be used and controlled. Manipulators know this, and they look for naïve individuals who may be willing and able to provide this for them.
- **Overly conscientious:** People who are highly conscientious care immensely about other people, and they give them far more consideration than they really should be. When it comes to being willing to give the manipulator the benefit of the doubt, there can be serious problems. There can be issues with all sorts of things if you don't know what you are looking for. In particular, you are able to expect to see that there are several problems when you are constantly giving other people the benefit of the doubt, but they are not willing to return the favor.
- **Low self-confidence:** Another thing to consider is the idea of low self-confidence. Manipulators see this as a mark of an easy target, and if you find yourself falling for this, you will realize that ultimately, you run into all sorts of issues that you will have to address. Your self-confidence, or lack thereof, could lead to situations in which manipulators find themselves taking total control.
- **Overthinking:** Sometimes, real vulnerability is the tendency to overthink things. The victim may find that they constantly attempt to understand why something happens the way that it does or how to better cope with it. The more that this is done, the more likely that it is that there will be other issues as well. When you consider this, you will see that these targets tend to allow for everything to pass by because they get so caught up in wondering whether they are overthinking the issue or not.
- **Emotional dependency:** Some victims are simply willing to risk everything for those around them. They will find

themselves feeling as if they must make it a point to get along with those around them. They choose to find ways that they would be able to continue to make sure that they are closely tied to those around them, and that means that they are oftentimes willing to forgive just about anything if it means that they get to maintain their position that they are in.
Typically, manipulators will look for an assortment of these traits or tendencies in their victims—they are able to spot these weaknesses, and they take control of them. They want to be able to utilize this tendency toward being able to control those around them, and they will do so in just about any way that they can manage to justify.

CHAPTER 4
Emotional Manipulation

Emotional manipulation is highly insidious—it is something that leaves no visible marks on its victims. It can leave people feeling controlled, confused, and sometimes, even as if they are worthless. It can slowly but surely destroy everything about someone else, holding them down and back. Have you ever found yourself feeling something that you could not quite explain? It could have been the result of emotional manipulation. Likewise, have you ever made it a point to figure out how you could begin to influence the emotions of those around you? This is also a form of emotional manipulation.

Within this chapter, we are going to address a few key concepts: We will first spend some time identifying and defining what emotional manipulation is. We will then go over several different types of emotional manipulation that are designed to take charge, take control, and get people doing what the manipulator wants them to do. If you learn to pay attention, you are able to start to see how this works—you are able to realize that you are more capable of figuring out how to control people than you may initially think. Or, you may learn that you are able to spot this form of manipulation with ease as well.

What Is Emotional Manipulation?

If you are going to utilize emotional manipulation, the first key consideration to remember is that emotional manipulation can undermine relationships, hurting the victim. This is something that you must consider—is this something that you are willing to do? Will you pay the price for this? If so, then keep reading. If not, no harm is done.

Emotional manipulation is designed to make sure that people are able to influence the emotions of someone else. Technically, by that definition, even a baby crying for food could technically be deemed emotional manipulation—it makes the mother want to stop the baby from crying. However, in the scope of this book, we are looking at acts that are deliberately self-serving for the manipulator—the acts are those that will directly influence and control the people and will lead to the reactions that the individual is looking for. It is commonly done in order to get one's own needs met, or sometimes, to achieve goals. However, so long as the manipulation is designed to influence the emotions of someone else, it officially falls under this bracket, and that is something that you will have to consider as well. You must make sure that you are in a position where you understand what you are doing before you begin—because this form of manipulation can cause serious harm if you do not know what you are doing.

Love Bombing and Devaluation

This first method of emotional manipulation that we will discuss is the idea of love bombing and devaluation. This exists in a cycle—the cycle involves first strongly addicting the target to the manipulator, and then occasionally making the target feel as if they do not matter or as if they are irrelevant. When you do this enough, you run into a situation in which the target, who is being fed intermittent reinforcement, grows closer. They try harder.

Typically, love bombing happens at the beginning of a new relationship of any kind—the idea is that the individual, every time he or she comes over, will leave behind presents, praise, or general words of kindness. This typically is piled on far quicker than most people would normally be willing to accept—but you assume that it is genuine and move on. You accept the love bombs, and you enjoy them. You'd think that this is the end of this story—but it is not.

Ultimately, love bombing is that act of promising that affection at first, and then, devaluation occurs when the target is completely and utterly tossed to the side. The idea is that in doing so, the target is going to want to be right back onto that point of a pedestal that he or she wants to do. This sort of emotional manipulation can then be used to try to sort of entice the individuals to continue looking at it.

Fear, Obligation, Guilt

When you use Fear, Obligation, and Guilt, you are making use of their key feelings that you sometimes have. These relationships that you build are not built upon the right foundations to help, and they may even cause significant trouble if you do not know what you are doing. However, the truth is, these three emotions are highly powerful. Fear motivates people to avoid things that might be dangerous. Obligation works by making people feel like they have no choice but to comply. Finally, guilt is a powerful motivator that we have that tells us not to ever repeat something again.

When you consider this method, then you will be working to influence and control the emotions of those around you. You might try to intimidate the individual, or you may have something else to say to them that will help them begin to fear the situation. Then, you may find that you choose to encourage a sense of obligation. You may do something for them, so they feel obligated to do the same when the time comes. This is perfect in getting what you want, as we will be addressing shortly.

Finally, let's talk about guilt. Guilt is the feeling that is there to drive people to never repeat the same mistakes again. It is there to remind the individual that they must change to be in a better situation. It is there, so you do not continue to do things that will hurt you or those around you.

When you put all three of these together, you have a very compelling source of information and control that you are able to continue to use if you need it. By taking this control for yourself, you are able to begin to control other people as a result.

The Silent Treatment

The silent treatment is not usually thought of as emotional abuse, but it Is time to identify what is meant when you are talking about the silent treatment. The silent treatment is this point in which one or two partners refuse to speak to the other one. Maybe they disagreed on where to go out to dinner and ended up insulting the taste of the other. Neither party was able to find an agreement that was satisfied, and as a result, they voted nothing. They did not upvote or downvote. They were not there to cause problems with the election or to do anything other than carefully but subtly do their thing.

The problem with the silent treatment is that it is, well, silent. It involves refusing to speak—it involves being willing to simply not communicate due to selfishness or due to not wanting to get involved in something. However, it is also highly effective if you absolutely must get a job done. It will help you to do that much at the very least.

To use the silent treatment, all you have to do is remain silent when someone else is talking to you. By remaining silent and refusing to engage, you are utilizing this method.

Gaslighting

Finally, the last method that we will briefly look at in this chapter is the idea of gaslighting. Gaslighting is the idea in which you will attempt to convince someone else that they cannot perceive reality around them. The idea is to make them feel so concerned, so out of power, and so out of touch with everything around them that they begin to rely on their partner's perceptions as well. At first, it starts out innocently enough—you might notice that something is not where you left it, or you may find that you are questioning what you did and your partner says something else. However, one thing has been found: This form of manipulation can be highly dangerous.

Using this begins with building up trust and then carefully working your way to ensuring that you have that control that you are looking for. Through gaslighting, you will start to deny small things. If your partner says they left their keys on top of the table, perhaps you find them on the floor next to the counter instead. You slowly do this over time—usually over a week or two—and you slowly but surely manage to mark off every instance of what you are doing and how you need to change. You will start to accept what the other person wants you to do and you will have no problems simply deferring to him or her. Over time, this eventually erodes further into what you know as manipulation today. When this happens, you see the fullest effects of the gaslighting, and as a result, you may find yourself in utter control of someone else, or you are able to get and maintain that control as well if you know what you are doing.

Either way, gaslighting becomes something that is dangerous if it is in the wrong hands. Gaslighting is highly important for just about anyone to have an understanding of, and without it, you will struggle. Keep in mind that while at first, this is little more than a table game. However, over time, it gets bigger and bigger. You could see that your target will take your word as a rule and will always follow. Alternatively, you could wind up biting off more than you think you are able to chew.

CHAPTER 5
Mind Control

Do you wish that you could influence or control someone else? Have you ever wondered if you could just find some way to influence what other people are doing with ease? Do you wish that with a simple snap of your fingers, you could properly influence the way that you engage with other people? While you cannot simply take control of someone else in the sense that you may be thinking, you do have the ability to heavily influence the way that they think. You are able to begin to influence how people behave by controlling those thoughts in their own way. All you have to do is be willing to see it your way and go forward.

In this chapter, we are going to take a look at a few different ways that manipulators are able to control the minds of those around them. Being able to control someone else's mind is something that is highly powerful. It is something that you are able to utilize in all sorts of different ways that will allow you to do so much more. Through being able to do so, you will find that you actually have far more control than you realize. Controlling the minds of everyone around you will allow you to take that control that you were looking for. Being able to understand what is going on and when it is happening, you will be able to see precisely what you need to do to take control.

What Is Mind Control?

First, it is important to note what mind control is *not*. It is not something that will grant you utter control over what someone does. You will not likely be able to simply tell them, "Go do this now" and get good results. However, what it will do for you is grant you that ability to better understand what they are doing and why they do things the way that they do. You are not just magically controlling people, as the name may imply, but you will be able to influence how that person sees the world around them. When you learn how to utilize mind control, you are able to make sure that you speak or act in ways that will help you directly learn how to influence them. You learn what it will take for you to make sure that they are behaving in ways that benefit you.

You are controlling thoughts and feelings in hopes of influencing behaviors when you utilize mind control, and by doing so properly, you will find that you are able to actually make major progress in how you engage with people. You are able to start to convince them of what they need to do and how they should do it. You are able to make sure that they know what it is that you need from them so that they can feel like you do understand them. You want to make sure that ultimately, you are talking to them in ways that will motivate them.

Mind control works primarily because your thoughts will influence your feelings, and your feelings will influence your behaviors. In particular, we are talking about unconscious thoughts here—the thoughts that you are entirely unaware of. Your unconscious or subconscious thoughts are those that you are not actively thinking, but that influence you nonetheless. In particular, when you have these thoughts, they are controlling you from the background without you having to do anything at all. When you utilize this process, you are doing so because the unconscious mind is constantly paying attention to the world around you. Your unconscious mind will always naturally tune in to things around you so that it can pay closer attention to the world around you without you having to also be aware of it. It allows you to save that awareness for when you really need it. Keep in mind that your mind is something that should not be taken lightly. If you are going to control the mind of someone else, then make sure that you do so tactfully.

With that cycle of thoughts, feelings, and behaviors, you ought to see that controlling the minds of those around you becomes quite simple for you. You simply must learn to pay attention to that never-ending cycle. This loop will help you to influence people: It allows you to start to shortcut—to take the thoughts of someone else and apply them to what you are doing. If you do this enough, you will get great at spotting what you must do.

Types of Mind Control

When it comes time to identify how mind control works, you must also understand that there are several different ways that you are able to use it. If you want to be able to control the other person, you will usually use one of the very predictable forms of mind control to make sure that you get that power over them. When you have that, you are able to start to actually piece it all together and make it happen.

Isolation

The first method that we will consider is isolation. When people are in isolation, they will suffer. We are a social species, and with that comes the inherent need to crave connection to other people. We naturally require other people to be around us so that we can thrive. We are not meant to be kept alone without other people. When you do isolate someone else, you start to control who they are around. Through being the only point of contact that person has, you are then able to start directly and significantly influencing their mind. This is relevant here—if you want to control other people, you must make sure that you are taking control of how they see themselves as well. This is precisely how cults tend to take control—they isolate their followers so that they have no choice but to accept what they are doing and being stuck with where they are. They start to believe everything that is said about them, and over time, they accept the cult ideology, completing the process.

Through isolating someone else, you are able to wear them down easier over time. You are able to start instilling that doubt in that person—they will start to think that no, they are not fully capable of thinking or acting accordingly. When you do this, you are working to properly take control of the other person.

To isolate someone, you must first be able to develop a good relationship with them. You must be able to get into a position of trust so that you are able to start to take that control in the first place. You are able to do this in several different ways, such as utilizing your body language to become an authority figure or working to make it sound like you are the individual's only ally in the situation, which is a tactic that you will also see during brainwashing when we get to that chapter. The more that you do this, the more likely you are to successfully get the other person to listen.

Essentially, through isolating them, you are able to develop enough trust that you will be the primary point of control. If they need an opinion about something, if you have isolated them from everyone else, the only place that they can go is to you. That is something that you are able to use to help yourself in control and in power in this situation. As you do this, you slowly plant the seeds of what you want them to be and how you want them to think. The more that you manage to succeed at this, the more likely that you are to actually maintain that mind control that you are looking for. To isolate someone, you have a few different options:

1. Physical isolation in which you restrict the movements of the other person to keep them within your grasp so that you are able to control all external resources and maintain complete control over the situation and individual.
2. Mental isolation, in which you make them feel like they are alone, whether they are or not. You could be blocking phone calls or intercept letters or messages. You send the idea that nobody cares and that they are truly alone, making them easier to control.
3. Censorship, in which you start to limit the influence of the outside world. You make it so that there is as little contact with the world around them as possible. By doing this, you are capable of influencing the only direct contact that person gets to the world.

Criticism

Criticism is an attempt to indirectly control everything around the other person so that they feel like they are ground down and want to give in to everyone else. When it comes time to be capable of controlling the other person, you want to make them feel like everything that they do is under complete scrutiny. This is perfect for taking control of the other person.

Through your ability to nit-pick at the other person, criticizing them at every chance that is afforded to you, you start to build that sense of doubt within them. They start to feel like they are the ones that are problematic instead of you. They assume that you are not the problem because they naturally trust you and what you are doing and saying. The more that you are capable of covertly criticizing them, the more likely that you are to get that desired result that you were looking for.

For example, imagine that you want your partner to get a better job. You might mention that you wish that he had a job that made more money. You may choose to mention that you wish that there was a way that you could afford something more. You might point out how your friends' partners are starting to make more money, and you wish that your partner was as well. You want them to feel like they are in a position where they are going to be criticized for what they are doing and how they are doing it. The more that you are able to push this point of criticism, the more likely that you are to find a way to cause problems. There are all sorts of ways that you are able to do this, but it all boils down to simply using shame to control the other person. You are trying to make the other person feel bad about themselves so that they are willing to give in to what you want. You make them feel like the only way for them to fix their problem is if they actually make it a point to change up the entire situation and do what you wanted from them in the first place.

Peer pressure

Through peer pressure, you are able to also control people. Remember, no one wants to be alone, and no one wants to feel as if they are stuck or unable to get past a situation because of how they behave. They want to fit in—if they feel like they do not fit in, they often want to comply with fixing the problem as soon as possible. This means that through utilizing peer pressure, you are able to actually sort of influence how people choose to behave. Through this sort of influence, you are capable of getting people to do just about anything. All you have to do is make sure that you put things in the light of you want them to do something because it is what everyone else is doing.

You could, for example, make sure that the individual is primarily surrounded by only other people that do what you want them to do, utilizing isolation as well as this sort of peer pressure to control the other person. You could also simply appeal to statistics that prove the stance that you are taking in which people have no choice but to admit that yes, things do have to go a certain way.

Repetition

Finally, you are able to also make use of repetition to control the other person as well. When you make use of repetition, you will be able to start putting ideas into the mind of the other person to control them. Remember, the mind is constantly listening, and because of this, you will be able to identify how the mind always pays attention to its surroundings. This means that over time, your unconscious mind will absorb information that could be used to control it as well. This is information about, for example, what your mind is doing at any point in time. You could also control the other person by repeating the same message over and over again in different contexts. This is effectively subliminally attempting to assert control over someone else—you are counting on them, not realizing that their unconscious mind is absorbing that opinion little by little. The more that this is done, the less likely that they are to properly fight the point in the first place. This method, of course, requires tact and some degree of covert attitude to the whole situation. You must make sure that you are working well to make sure that they will not pick up on the repetition, but that it will be absorbed in other ways.

Think about it—you could be making it a point to repeat a point about a book or movie or even an unpopular opinion about something. The more that you reiterate this point, whether they are aware of it or not, the more that you will start to plant that message to them. Think about how often we look at what is happening around us. Consider just how often we tend to do things in a certain way because of sheer repetition as well. The more that you recognize and tap into this, the more likely that you are to successfully plant that idea in the first place.

CHAPTER 6
Neuro-Linguistic Programming

Next, let's take some time to go over neuro-linguistic programming. NLP is a common way in which you will be able to start influencing the minds of other people solely because you are capable of understanding the relationships between the body and mind. Through tapping into those relationships, you are able to start to work out truths and even heal from traumas over time. It is highly potent, powerful, and is even easy to learn. The initial purpose behind NLP was to provide something that the average person could learn to teach themselves or those closest to themselves about how they can move on in life or change themselves to be successful. Now, while it has the potential to be abused, NLP is also something that can really do a lot of good for people, especially if they regularly see a practitioner. It becomes something that they can utilize to help themselves, and they often find that it is highly influential as well. If you want to make use of NLP, you must recognize the truth: That there are these massively important ways that you are able to interact with the world.

Keep in mind that, though NLP and mind control shares some similarities, this is not actually the case. NLP is meant to be built upon a solid relationship with the other person—it is meant to create rapport through mirroring with the other person. This idea is that the mirror neurons between yourself and the other party will be strong enough that you feel that intense chemistry. That chemistry is known as rapport, and rapport will help you immensely in life. Rapport will help you to tap into what you want—it will allow you to properly influence and control the way that the other person is thinking so that you are able to influence and control them as well.

Just like with mind control, you will be utilizing the same cycle of thoughts, feelings, and behaviors. You will be influencing the way that the people act through influencing their unconscious thoughts. The idea is that your conscious and unconscious minds are not able to fully communicate with each other- they both exist separately from each other. However, through actions, they are able to communicate. Your unconscious mind is able to create feelings that influence your behaviors, and when you use NLP, you are influencing the unconscious mind of someone else.

What Is NLP?

Designed so anyone can do it without requiring psychology training, NLP is a method of influence in which you are able to communicate with the unconscious mind of someone else to influence their behaviors. It effectively allows you to use your own body language and actions to directly influence the unconscious mind of someone else so that you are able to then see precisely what they are doing. Through this indirect attempt to influence the other person, you then get that control. You learn to control them through controlling their unconscious mind. This is done through vocabulary, actions, and more. Little by little, you will use your own actions to directly influence the other person.

All that matters is that they must sense what you are doing. You are able to influence any of the senses—sight, sounds, taste, smell, or touch can allow you to directly influence the mind. You are able to make certain tastes or smells trigger certain thoughts to control a reaction, for example, or you could also make it so that the individual is going to respond to certain words a certain way. This sort of conditioning allows you to take control of that person with ease. All you have to do is make sure that you are in full control of the situation.

NLP works because people have a way that they all see the world, and that way is very distinct. That way that they see the world is something that can be altered. Remember, how you see the world and interpret it is subjective, not objective. That subjectivity is something that is easily altered. You are able to start to change the mindset that other people take about something relatively simple. All you have to know is how to present it to rewrite that map of reality. Once you actively tap into their mind and change how they choose to behave, you are able to maintain control over the other party. The more that you do this, the easier it will become. All you have to do is encourage the thought, feeling, or action that you want them to begin using, and everything else will follow.

Mirroring, Rapport, and NLP

Before you are able to begin to utilize NLP, however, you must first develop a rapport with the other person. This is the reputation that you hold with the other person. It is the measure of the relationship that you and the other person share—it is the way that you both communicate in an effective manner. When you and the other person have a rapport with each other, you are on good terms—you are on the same page, and you will also be working together more. This is something that can be seen at a glance when you see other people wandering around with each other. If you want to identify people with good rapport with each other, you must take a look at how they engage with the person that they are with.

When people have a rapport with each other, they both mirror each other. Mirroring refers to what happens when two people follow each other's movements. Imagine how you see friends walking alongside each other at the same pace, with their steps happening at the same time. They also may take a drink at the same time, or they might move about together. If one person touches their head, the other will do so as well, or when one person shifts, the other follows. This happens because when we view someone doing something else, similar areas in the brain will go off as well. However, the part that goes off is not the same part that causes you to do the same thing. It is the part of your brain that helps you to empathize with them. This is what works well to allow for people to relate to others.

Mirroring is something that happens naturally most of the time, but it is also something that you are able to force as well if you do not have the time to start developing the relationship with others. If you want to make sure that you are capable of triggering that rapport from other people but are short on time, you have options.

Perhaps one of the most common ways to do so involves taking a few minutes to mirror the other person first. Because the unconscious mind is always paying attention, being able to mirror someone else first cues to them that you are mirroring them. This then triggers this concept of reciprocity—their body will naturally follow along as well, and that is highly important as well. When that happens, you start to see that they are actually far more interested in following along. This is because they almost feel compelled to do so- -they feel like they are required to follow along even though they may not actually have that relationship set in stone yet.

Mirroring, then, is one of the most important skills that you are able to develop if you hope to be capable of managing the way that you interact with other people. If you want to be able to control others, then you must make sure that you are able to influence them your own way, and that includes being capable of watching how you engage. Mirroring follows a few simple steps when you need to do it, all of which are incredibly easy to manage.

1. **Attention:** It all begins with attention. Make the other person the center of your world, so you are able to properly develop a pseudo-relationship with them. You want to be fully convinced that you like them if you want them to like you in return. See them as the most important person for you to talk to at the moment, face them, and make eye contact as you listen to them.
2. **Mimicking:** Next comes the mimicking stage. Now, many sources will tell you to follow the body language, taking their poses and movements, or drinking when they drink, but if you are not naturally following each other, they are much more likely to see that you are doing it at the moment and that can cause you problems. If they catch that you are deliberately following their body language, they will be much less likely to like you—they will simply think that you are weird or untrustworthy, and that is highly problematic. Instead, mimic their vocal cues. This will allow you to follow their nonverbal communication without being visually

obvious. Due to differences in the way that voices sound, they are much less likely to notice if you are simply following along with their body language than if you were doing something else. This means you should follow how they speak. Listen to how they tend to pace themselves. Pay attention to the tone and the excitement level in their voice. Match it and keep pace with them. Their unconscious mind will notice, even if consciously, they entirely miss the point.

3. **Seal the deal:** The third step requires you to seal the deal by tapping into the punctuator. The punctuator is something that is used by people whether they realize it or not. The punctuator is the way that you will accentuate what you are doing at any point in time. Some people have a phrase they use when they are speaking. Other people choose to move a certain way as they engage with someone. Some people still waggle their eyebrows, or they smirk or smile. This is important—and you should be able to figure out what it is that they are doing every time they do. Listen for their punctuator, and when you figure it out, you will then need to copy it. You want to copy it for them the next time they are getting ready to say something. By beating them to the punch, you are able to seal the deal. They may not catch that you are copying them, but they will feel like you are paying close attention to them, and that will help to trigger them to feel that connection as well.

4. **Test:** Finally, all you have to do is test it. See if that connection is present there. You want to make sure that they have that connection with you before you attempt anything else. Try moving slightly—you could move yourself to the left and see if they shift to the left as well. You want to see if they are shifting around with you so that you are able to begin to tell what they think. If they follow along with you with small movements, then there is a good chance that they have that rapport built with you. That is a great sign for you—that means that you have succeeded. If not, you will need to start over and try again. If you cannot get through to them and convince them to follow you after a few attempts, then you will need to let go of the idea that you will actually get them to mirror back.

Following these steps will help you to develop that connection with other people so that you are able to influence them over time. When you have that mirroring established and they are following your actions, you will then be able to influence them simply by tapping into their body language.

Anchoring With NLP

Anchoring is just one of the many ways that you are able to utilize NLP. Anchoring is effectively allowing yourself to connect to other people. When you anchor someone to something, you will be able to influence them to have a conditioned response every time that they do something. Effectively, you will be able to move or prevent something from someone, and they will then trigger that response every time. This will allow you to control the behaviors of someone else, and it can go in several different ways. You could, for example, start by encouraging someone to feel like they must listen whenever you hold your hand a certain way. This is a good way to convince people to follow you if you are looking for obedience. You could also choose to utilize anchoring for yourself to remind yourself to stay assertive or to make sure that you are calm if you are an anxious person. Through anchoring yourself with a certain item, action, or thought, you will be able to calm yourself down as well. This is imperative if you want to be able to influence other people. Thankfully, anchoring is incredibly simple—you just have to follow a few simple steps.

1. **Identify what you want to condition:** First, you must figure out what it is that you want to trigger whenever you want it. Do you want them to feel a certain way? To concede in a confrontation every time? Figure out what it is.
2. **Identify your stimulus:** Then, you must also know what it is that you want to use to trigger in the other person. You want to be able to figure out how you are able to convince them to do what you need. It could be that you use a certain movement. You might want a certain word that you will use.
3. **Trigger the reaction:** To begin the conditioning process, you must first find a way to make them think or do what you were thinking. For example, imagine that you want to make someone apologize at a whim. You want to do something that will make the other person apologize to you. Maybe you make it so that they bump into you. Then, they will naturally apologize.
4. **Use the stimulus immediately after:** Then, as soon as you get that reaction, it is time to use the stimulus. You may use a certain hand gesture as they say that they are sorry.
5. **Repeat:** You will need to repeat this several times, but with time, you will start to conditionally respond to them. Over

time, you will start getting them to apologize just by moving that certain way in an argument or when you want them to do something.

This works because you simply condition them over time, little by little, to get them to properly follow along with you and what you are doing or what you want them to do. This is perfect if you want to condition someone else, so you are able to control them.

Weasel Words With NLP

The last form of NLP that we will look at here is the utilization of weasel words. This will allow you to communicate with people and convince them to do things just by how you speak to them. By changing up the way that you speak to the other person, you will be able to properly influence the other person. This is a great option for you if you want to know how to speak to people to get the reaction that you are looking for.

Effectively, you are leading the thought processes that someone else has by making sure that you phrase your questions and statements in a way that will naturally start to influence their thinking or worldview. This is effective in many ways. If you want to be able to tell them what to do or how to do it, you must make sure that you do so in an effective manner. You must make sure that as you engage with other people, you do so in a way that will allow you to help everyone involved. You must make sure that you think carefully about what you say so that you are able to convince them properly.

You start with questions that naturally lead to what you want them to do. For example, instead of asking if someone would like to buy something, you ask when they will buy. This shift in language makes their mind believe that buying is already determined and that they have nothing to think about. Rather, they must buy because there is no other choice. This is perfect to shift the focus, altering the unconscious mind, which then assumes that it *is* buying just because of the way that you spoke to it. This is perfect if you want to be able to convince people to purchase things or if you want or need to influence how people engage with others. You could also use language such as:

- After you...
- As you...
- When you notice...
- You may experience...
- You may realize...

With these ambiguous phrases, you slowly influence the mind of the other person to accept and appreciate what you had to say. Through doing so, you allow yourself that utter control over them, which is highly influential for you. The more that you are able to do this, the better. That vague ambiguity will grant you the ability to ride on plausible deniability without them realizing what you are doing at any point in time. There are really just a few key points to remember when you choose to use weasel words: You must make sure that you speak something that is a command with the tonality that shows a command as well. Through doing so, you should get them to unconsciously absorb what you say to them.

For example, maybe you are trying to sell a car to someone. You may say, "When you buy this, you will notice that it runs really well." Notice how you embedded that command—"You will." This is the key here. What you have said is all things considered, quite simply not offensive. However, you will also notice that there is more to it. The very way that it is phrased is done in such a way that it will influence them.

CHAPTER 7
Body Language

Body language is another powerful way that you are able to use to compel people to follow along with what you want them to do. It can be used in several different ways to get people to influence and control what they want or need. When you are able to understand the body language of other people, you are able to start to figure out what it is that you are able to do to influence other people as well. Because we see the body language of other people when we approach them, or when they approach us, we respond to it. This is why being approached warmly by a friend or family member can leave you feeling good while being approached by someone that is not so kind will actually lead you to feel nervous or even defensive or aggressive.

Through tapping into body language, you are able to start to influence other people as well. They will see what you are doing, and they will then alter their own behaviors to reflect upon that. You will influence other people simply by knowing how other people's minds work, once again tapping into that cycle of thoughts, feelings, and behaviors. When you are good at paying attention to these things, you are able to start recognizing just how likely it is that you are able to alter how they behave and what they do.

Remember, body language is powerful for a reason. We rely on it heavily, and we utilize it without ever thinking about it. However, you are able to also willingly and intentionally tap into it to begin to change how other people behave as well. This is imperative—the more that you alter how you respond and engage with other people, the better. This allows you to better influence how you are seen and helps you to be in control of a situation. When you are able to assert yourself as the dominant one, you are able to usually influence how those around you engage with you. Through doing this, you are able to then maintain control over the other person. You are effectively looking to use your body language to influence how the other person engages with you in hopes of being able to control them more thoroughly than you otherwise would be able to. Through doing this the right way, you maintain that air of confidence and control.

Leading Body Language

When you want your body language to lead other people, there are a few key ways that you are able to move yourself to ensure that the other parties around you see yourself that way. You do not have to do much to make yourself appear confident enough to be a leader—you just have to engage the right way to maintain that degree of leadership. If you play your cards right, you will find that you are highly successful at that level of influence that you are looking for. To lead with body language, consider the following to change your own movements to take control:

- **Maintain eye contact:** By ensuring that your eye contact is maintained, you are able to be confident as an individual. However, you must hold that eye contact with the other person in a way that is gentle rather than dominant or overbearing. You are not trying to come across as intimidating—you are looking for a way that you are able to relate to them more clearly. You are showing them that you listen to them and therefore, are giving them the attention that they deserve without being intimidated or uncomfortable by the process.
- **Stand tall:** When you keep your body language tall and open, standing up with your spine straight and keeping your head level with the other person, you are seen as confident enough to be a leader. The key here is that you do not want to be looking down your nose at the other person—you want to ensure that you stay straight with them. If you are able to do this, you are able to maintain that semblance of confidence that you are looking for.
- **Release tension:** Make sure that you are not tense when you are looking at the person that you are trying to lead or influence. You want to make sure that the calmness that you exude shows the confidence that you have.
- **Maintain open body language:** To have open body language is to be capable of showing that you are open to being engaged with by people around you. It is a relaxed body language that shows that you are non confrontational and that you are willing to engage; however, you must deal with those around you. Make sure that you do not cross your arms or put something in front of yourself.
- **Use your hands:** When you talk with your hands, you show that you are confident enough to keep your hands visible at all times. Doing so helps you to properly engage with those around you. It also helps you to avoid falling into traps, such as fidgeting with your hands or hiding them in your pockets.

Dominant Body Language

When it comes to having dominant body language, you intimidate other people into following you instead of convincing them that they want to, the way you would with a leadership type body language. Through domination, you are able to control the situation in an authoritarian manner. To dominate a situation, you want to ensure that you are as big as possible to other people. You want to make sure that you are in control rather than anyone else, and through doing so, you show that you control it all. Consider the following body language:

- **Keep a wide stance:** When your stance is wider, you show that you are not afraid to take up space. When your stance is wider, you show that you are more dominant just because you do take up the world around you. You want to be as big as possible, and this is the best starting point.
- **Keep hands on hips:** By putting your hands on your hips, you make yourself larger as well. You are controlling how you are seen by making yourself puff up larger.
- **Head up with the chin high:** When you do this, holding your head up with your chin tilted out, you make yourself larger than they are. Through doing this, you look down at the other party, which makes them feel like you are larger or taller than them.
- **Spread your stuff out:** When you spread out all of your stuff, you start to claim the space all around yourself as well. Through doing this, you show that you are more dominant because you claim more than what is around you. When you do this enough, encroaching on other people's space, you are able to show that you want to take control.
- **Touch other people's things:** When you start touching other people's things, you start to declare dominance over them too. You show them that you are claiming ownership of things that you touch as you go.
- **Walk along the center of a path:** When you push yourself through the center of a path without making space for other people, you show that you are the dominant one. You make it clear that you will not move because you do not need to. This allows for that declaration of dominance without having to do much at all. When you do this, you show that you will not share space.
- **Stare at other people:** When you stare at someone else intensely, you will be able to declare dominance over other people. Through staring at people, you make them more uncomfortable, and through doing so, you are able to declare that domination.

CHAPTER 8
Persuasion

Persuasion is another way that you are able to take control of other people, and it will allow you to convince other people to do what you want. When you persuade other people, you convince them to do what you want them to do. It is meant to be a bit more overt—when you speak to the people that you are trying to convince, you will be able to influence them simply because you persuade them.

Persuasion becomes a way for you to word things just right, phrasing your argument in convincing manners that will help you to get others to agree with you. Through the power of persuasion, you are able to get people to do whatever you could want them to. Think about how expert salespeople can convince someone to buy just about anything when they are good at their job—that is through sheer persuasion. Through utilizing the power of persuasion, they can tell people something and have that idea go through just right to influence the other party. This is a skill that just about everyone must master to some degree or another. Through mastering it, you are able to then begin to take control: You are able to persuade people into taking that skillset and utilize it for yourself. Through knowing what you are doing, you are able to ensure that what you say goes with ease. All you have to do is know a few key principles to follow along.

In this chapter, we will address two major points: The principles of persuasion, as well as rhetoric. These are two different methods that you are able to use to persuade other people to do whatever it is that you wanted them to do so that you are able to take control of a situation. If you are able to utilize these effectively, you are able to be on top of just about anything. You will be more likely to succeed and more likely to maintain that degree of confidence if you know how to utilize persuasion. The best leaders are often the most persuasive, and this is a skill that is necessary for many different jobs and career lines.

The Principles of Persuasion

First, we will consider the principles of persuasion. These are six key ways that you are able to phrase what you say or the situation that you are in so that you are able to be compelling to the people around you. When you know what you are doing, you will be able to utilize these skills in ways that will allow you to lead a situation naturally. Keep in mind that persuasion is a bit different from traditional manipulation—when you persuade someone, you are putting everything in front of them to see. You are showing them what you must do and how you must do it. You are teaching them the ways that they can begin to see the world so that they come to the conclusion that you want them to. This is much more indirect than true manipulation just due to the fact that usually, you are controlling the other person primarily through the way that you frame the situation. If you know what you are doing, you will be able to influence people with ease.

These work because, ultimately, they shift and influence the subconscious mind. They work by directly altering the way that you look at or treat other people in powerful ways. There are six different options that you are able to use: Reciprocity, consistency, social proof, authority, liking, and scarcity. Each of these will work in different ways to get that end result you are looking for.

Reciprocity

Reciprocity refers to the idea that when someone does something for you, you return the favor. This is the concept of giving and getting, and it helps people in social settings. When we engage in reciprocity, we feel like we must return things to people after we receive something from them in return. It helps to keep societies and family units running and drives people to work together to get the situations that are desired. If you are a car salesperson, for example, you probably have people coming in and out of your dealership constantly. You are able to help to get prospective clients to buy simply by making sure that you provide them with something in return first. If you wanted to, for example, you could give them a free coffee or give their children that they have with them lollipops. Such a small gesture actually goes a long way.

You are able to see this used in other contexts too—oftentimes, people get gifts given to them when they sign up for things, and they utilize that gift or that offer of a gift to encourage people. When they give you a gift, you feel more obligated or compelled to sign up as well. This is essential to being a social species and helps everyone. If you want to use this, then make sure that before you ask someone to do anything, you give them something first.

Consistency

There is a rule of human behavior that states that once someone starts saying yes to something, they will continue to say yes after. Think about it—when someone asks you to do something, and you agree, doing something a bit more doesn't seem as big of a deal. Think about it—imagine that someone asks you to toss something in the garbage as you walk past their desk. If that happens, then you would probably say yes: After all, it would be unreasonable for you to say no to that. Then, after you've said yes to that, you may find that they ask you to also pass them a pen as you come back. You agree to do that too because it isn't unreasonable to ask. From there, you might also be asked to pick something else up or glance over some paperwork. This is important to keep in mind for future use.

Imagine this—you are trying to get through some negotiations, but the other person is unreasonably stubborn. What are you supposed to do? The easiest answer is that you would simply utilize the idea of consistency in commitments to get them to agree to what you want. When you have to negotiate with someone who is clearly uninterested in negotiations, the best thing for you to do is to ask them to do something simple for you. You might ask them to pass that pen next to them because doing so forces them to move to open up their own body language, and once they agree to that, you are able to slowly get them to agree to other things as well.

Social proof
One of the main points that have been repeated throughout the entire book reiterated for importance is that we are social animals by nature. People love to be wanted and needed. We need to feel like we belong somewhere, even if that is just with our own friends and family. We want to feel like we are able to relate to people or like we are accepted. This is our drive to be social with others. It is also a common form of social proof that can be used as well. If you want to make sure that you are in control of a situation, then you are able to ensure that you get that social proof through making sure that you are laying on that peer pressure.

Effectively, if you are using social proof, you will be convincing the other person that they ought to do things a certain way because that is the way that everyone else does it as well. By doing so, you can make use of pointing out how other people do what you want them to do. You can show them that ultimately if they want to be like everyone else, that is what they will need to do. They will need to find a way to relate to everyone else just because of the fact that they will be doing different things. When you do this effectively, you will learn that you can do more. You will discover that you are more than capable of convincing people of just about anything.

Imagine, for example, you want someone to buy a specific item. You tell them that they should want to buy that item specifically because you know that their hero or their favorite athlete buys that item. This is precisely what you see done when you see advertisers using famous sponsors for their product—they want to rely on that social proof to sell their products for them.

Authority
Authority is a simple principle to understand—this principle dictates that when given a choice, you will always defer to a perceived authority. Imagine that your car just broke down. You might search for how to fix it online, but if your neighbor comes up to you and says, "Hey, I'm a mechanic, and I'm pretty sure this is what is wrong with your car," you are quite likely to believe them. Because they positioned themselves in that frame of being an authority figure, you are more likely to defer to them.

This can commonly be used in sales positions or in positions in which you want your authority to be taken seriously. Imagine, for example, that you want to get someone to listen to you. You might be a consulter for something, for example. You might want to consider putting up testaments to your achievements in the room around you. Maybe you have degrees and accolades all around, hanging on the walls. Perhaps you have an award from that time you won the award for the best service. By putting up these signs that you have done well, you assert yourself as an authority figure so that you can be certain that everything works according to plan. When you do this, you will realize that you are setting yourself up to be an authority to get that power over them. This is imperative—you must be able to accept and embrace that power for yourself. Assert why you should be in charge and do not back down from it. Make it clear that you deserve it.

Liking
Another simple principle to utilize is the idea of liking. This principle states that if you like something or someone, you are more likely to say yes when asked to do something. Think about it—you are much more likely to go out of your way to help a good friend or family member that you like than of someone that you dislike. This is imperative to keep in mind: You want to make sure that people who you like are taken care of, and that usually translates into helping them when they ask you to. This means, then, that if you want to get help from someone else, you want to make sure that they like you as well. You need a way to assert yourself as someone that is likable to them so that they will feel compelled to help you somehow. This can happen in all sorts of different ways, depending upon what you want to do and how you do it. However, there are three criteria to be well-liked by people:

1. You must be seen as human to the other person. This is especially important if you are attempting to get someone to help you that you do not yet know. You want to make sure that they see you as personalized. You might try putting up pictures of your family or say how you can relate to the other person. You could relate to their car, what they are wearing, or even if you have children around the same age as the other person. These simple acts can help you to be seen as a person to the individual that you are interacting with, and by doing so, you can help yourself as well.
2. You must then make them feel good about themselves when you talk to them. You want to encourage those good feelings because they will then associate you with those good feelings. However, you must be mindful of the way that you do so—you cannot come across as if you are trying to butter them up. You must come across as genuine. Make sure that whatever you compliment is something that you genuinely like, so you do not have to lie to them about something. This is the best way to be effective with how you engage with them.
3. Finally, you must cooperate with them. Make sure that whatever the two of you are doing is suddenly a team effort. You can make this happen in all sorts of different ways. Encourage them to see

the situation as collaborative. Ask them to help you help them. This is a great way to make them relate to you and, therefore, like you more.

When you put those steps into place, you will be able to better influence them to like what is going on. It is highly effective in ensuring that they do want to help you out along the way, and if you can master how you do this, you can actually make great progress in getting them to be on your side.

Scarcity

Finally, the last principle of persuasion is that of scarcity. This simple principle tells you that there is more value when things are scarce than when they are plentiful. This makes perfect sense—if you want something that is hard to get, you will inherently value it higher than if it were easily acquired without much effort. This means that if you want to really get something from someone, you must ensure that you are on the right track. You must make sure that you choose out what you are doing and when you do it so that your time or your skills are scarce. You want to make them feel like they have to work to get what you are giving, or make them feel pressured.

This is precisely why so many salespeople will offer you a good deal and then put a short expiration on it. Perhaps you are trying to buy a house, and your realtor continually puts 24-hour limits on the offers—this is to pressure the individual to accept what you have offered up. If you want to be able to get a house, you want them to feel like your offer is not just sitting there idly for weeks at a time, tying up your money—you want that pressure there to encourage them to take it. Scarcity will work well to persuade people or push them toward a choice sooner rather than later, something that you may find that you really need as you continue forward.

Rhetoric and Persuasion

Beyond simple principles of persuasion, you should also recognize that persuasion can also be considered from a lens of rhetoric. This refers to the idea that your speech should also be persuasive. If you want to persuade others to do something, you must make sure that you do so the right way. This means making sure that you work through what you are doing and speak in certain ways. The best way to motivate people, then, is to use some sort of rhetorical appeal. In rhetoric, there are three appeals that a person can make: An appeal to character, an appeal to emotion, and an appeal to logic. Each works slightly differently and gets completely different results when you utilize them. All you have to do is know what you are doing.

Appeal to character

The appeal to character requires you to set yourself up as an authority figure of some sort. You want to find a way that you can frame yourself to be this authority so the other person feels like they must listen to you. It could be that you are experienced in what you are discussing. You could have gone through something that makes you uniquely qualified to talk about whatever you are discussing.

When you use this appeal, make sure that your discussion or speech to the other person focuses on what you have done that puts you in that position of being qualified to talk. You want to ensure that they see a reason to believe in you or what you are saying so that you are successfully able to discuss what is happening. This is oftentimes done through making a backstory that is highly compelling to the audience, or by explaining how you are capable of getting the results that you are looking for. By knowing what you are doing and making it happen, you can be certain that you will get what you want from the audience. They will be more likely to follow you if they feel that they have a good reason to.

Appeal to emotion

Appeals to emotion are a bit different—they are designed to make someone feel an emotion so that the emotion that is triggered can be used to influence the person. It could be that you add information through discussing an emotional event, or you try to point out something that happened when someone did not do what you wanted them to. Perhaps you say that the family that did not opt for the extra safety features on their car got into an accident, and everyone was seriously injured. Maybe you discuss how the last person to not follow your diet advice ended up with diabetes and getting a foot amputated. You want the stories that are used to evoke strong emotion because that strong emotion will then compel the behaviors that you are looking for from the person. You want them to feel the reasons that they should give you whatever you are looking for or asking for so that they do it.

Appeal to logic or reasoning

Finally, an appeal to logic is a form of persuasion that will throw logic, facts, and numbers at the individual in order to create an argument that is so compelling, the best thing that can be done is to accept it. These arguments, however, are rarely actually as logically sound as they are supposed to be. They are often skewed to try to get the individual to agree just to win the argument. Commonly, there will be a barrage of statistics that will be too overwhelming to parse through little by little, so the individual will simply choose to do as you have asked instead of trying to fight it or figure out what would work best for them. When people hear that there are factual reasons for them to follow what is being pushed, they are much more likely to agree just by default.

CHAPTER 9
Hypnosis

At this point, it is time to address the act of hypnosis as a form of influence over people. When you use hypnosis, you are capable of strongly influencing them through simply acting in certain ways. Hypnosis is not simply getting someone to go around clucking like a chicken—it is not waving a pendulum to get utter compliance. Rather, it is the act of getting someone into a state of gentle suggestiveness so that they are willing to accept your suggestions and act upon them. It is not closing off one's mind or shutting it down—it is actually a point of hyper-focusing. It is there to cause the mind to focus so intently on just one thing that it feels as if they are not all there. This is because their mind is stuck on whatever it is that they are focusing on.

It is not instantaneous, nor is it something that puts someone to sleep. In fact, they are actually going to be incredibly awake during these trance states. Hypnosis is defined as a trance-like state in which the individual is open to suggestions, relaxed, and heightened in imagination as well. There is a degree of hyper-focus and alertness that leads to ignoring just about everything in your surroundings, despite the fact that you will be completely conscious.

When you hypnotize someone else, you set them up so that they are entirely willing to accept your suggestions. You will feel or think whatever you are told. If you hypnotize someone and then tell them that they have a bag of lead on them so they cannot move, they will believe you, even if nothing is there. They will be entirely convinced that they cannot move, and they will remain there. When you encourage this state of mind, then, you are given direct access to the unconscious mind that you can use to control the rest of the thoughts that someone has.

Essentially, hypnosis works because of the fact that it will fast-track information straight to your unconscious mind. Remember, you are fully aware of what is in your consciousness, but not the unconscious. If you are trying to influence someone to feel like they must do something, then you want to do so through getting to their unconscious in the first place. You want to suggest things to it so that they will be more willing to act them out in the first place. This means that you are fully expecting the individual to relax into a state where anything that you say is going to naturally be absorbed into the mind. You want them to figure out how they can talk to you in a way that will allow for this.

As you get into that state of suggestibility, you get to a point in which you are not inhibited by your conscious thought. Your conscious mind is highly logical—it is the part of your mind that is there to influence you or make you feel like you are inhibited. It is the part of your mind that tells you that dancing on top of that ledge on top of a cliff is a dangerous idea and that you should probably avoid doing so. When you hypnotize someone, however, you can suggest that they should dance on that ledge, they probably feel like it is a good idea. They will absorb those thoughts or suggestions right into their subconscious, and as a result, they will fall for exactly what you have suggested from them. If you do this the wrong way, you will find that you fail.

While many people doubt that hypnosis is a real thing, it has been backed by science on more than one occasion. The body's vital signs do not really change much during the state of hypnosis, but it is the case that the brain's activity does change notably and significantly during these states. It has been found through electroencephalographs (EEGs) that during hypnosis, wave frequency is lowered. This is what commonly is also found during dreaming states in terms of brain activity. At the same time, the higher frequency waves, usually associated with alertness, are dropped. This allows for the support that the conscious mind is actively subdued during periods of hypnosis to allow for the subconscious mind to be so accessible.

There have also been studies done under hypnosis that show that activity is reduced within the left hemisphere's cerebral cortex. It is then increased on the right side, which is the part of the brain that rules imagination and creativity. By inhibiting activity in the left hemisphere, the conscious mind's logical nature is suppressed, while the increase of activity on the right side implies that there are more creative aspects focused upon.

All of this implies that there is a very real phenomenon known as hypnosis, and it absolutely is effective in its own ways. Through being able to understand this process effectively, you can then start to utilize it as well. Now, let's consider a few different types of hypnosis to begin understanding the process of using it.

Hypnotizing Through Speech

First, let's consider hypnosis through speech. When you want to hypnotize someone without them catching on, you can usually do so through the word choice that you utilize. Using words that will heavily imply relaxation can often work well for this, much like what you would expect with NLP methods of influence on people. If you want to trigger that state of influence in someone, you must make sure that you lead with the right kind of language that will then encourage those feelings or thoughts that you want them to utilize.

In hypnosis, you must trigger a state of relaxation, and with this, you will start encouraging it through progressive relaxation and imagery. Through utilizing your voice instead of tools, you can usually encourage calmness. If you have ever listened to a guided meditation that has been narrated before, you have been hypnotized by the gentle nature of speech that you heard. The best way to get it to work is to use a low and soothing voice, much like if you were trying to shush and lull a baby to sleep. If you can make this happen the right way, you can then encourage the individual to feel much more relaxed.

As you speak, you must command their absolute attention. You must make sure that they are listening to you so you can get them to follow along into that suggestive state. As you continue to speak, you must suggest relaxing. This can be done by discussing just how calming it would be to do something. Maybe you mention softly that it is so peaceful to watch those apple blossoms blow off of the apple tree in your front yard, watching them fall one by one down the path. Maybe you talk about the gentle nature of the river as it flows downstream or the quiet softness of falling snow. As you slowly and calmly speak, you lull the other person into a state of relaxation as well. Through doing so, willing minds will then naturally start to relax as well. You will trigger that trance-like state that you are looking for, and in that state, you can then influence them to get them to do whatever it is that you were looking for from them.

Hypnotizing With Movements

When you want to hypnotize someone through movements, you are doing something similar to when you are speaking. However, this time, you are drawing upon your ability to mirror someone else, and then you are slowly easing them into following your own repetitive movements with ease. You want them to follow along so that you can be certain that they are on the same page as you and so that they will naturally follow your actions as well. Think about how when you rock an infant to sleep, they are quickly soothed by the motion, and how it is possible for you to do the same to yourself. How many people fall asleep in rocking chairs or on the long car ride home when they are a passenger? It can be easy to fall asleep if you do not have anything keeping you from doing so.

Movements can be incredibly relaxing to help you ease into that state of mind in which you can influence other people. All you have to do is make sure that as you move, you will be able to tap into what you want. You might be able to gently sway as you discuss something with someone else, encouraging them to do the same. This will then cause them to relax more, and as they begin to relax more, they will naturally follow along with what you ask of them. They will start feeling much more inclined to do what you want as you ask them to do something.

Hypnotizing Through Repetitive Sounds

Finally, you can also induce a state of hypnosis through a droning voice that is quite repetitive as well. Think back to your time in school. Did you ever feel like you were falling asleep just by listening to what other people around you were saying? This is caused by hypnosis—or at least, a similar premise. Though your teacher may not have intentionally tried to hypnotize you, they did so through their droning, repetitive voice that did not vary much. This, done without any fluctuations at all in pitch, voice, or speed, can be mind-numbing, and as a result, it leads to people who are not really paying much attention. It triggers that desire to daydream or that lack of attention to what is going on around them. This is a great way for you to take control of someone else without them ever being aware of it.

This is a bit harder to do naturally because if you talk with a flat drone, most people will question you. However, if you know what you are doing, you can bore the mind of the other person into submission, allowing you to start adding in what you want them to do into your script after a while. This is actually a common method that is used in indoctrinating people into cults. You make it a point to drone on as much as possible to control the other person, and as a result, you capture their minds and their efforts. This is highly useful if you know what you are doing.

CHAPTER 10
Reverse Psychology

When we were in school, we all tried out reverse psychology at one point or another. Reverse psychology becomes this exciting thing for people when they realize that it often works far better than most people expect it to—when you are exposed to reverse psychology, you often feel like you are caught up in something that forces you to do something. It is something that happens mostly toward children, but if done well, it can actually utilize the psychological phenomenon known as reactance.

Reactance is the negative reaction to trying to be persuaded. It is that defiant attitude that people often take when someone tries to get them to do something or that attitude that tells the other person that they have no choice but to do something or attempt something. Through reactance, you can run into all sorts of problems. You want to make sure that you can limit this—but sometimes, you can use it to your advantage if you know how to push it a bit further. You would simply want to make sure that you are a step ahead of the other person. If you know, for example, that someone is quite reactive or volatile when you try to get them to do something, you might want to use that to your advantage. This could be, for example, trying to tap into someone's resistant nature to give indirect orders.

For the vast majority of people, direct orders are good enough. However, there are many people out there that require this indirect approach to sort of guide them into that reaction that you are looking for. This is somewhat paradoxical—the resistant people fall for this sort of manipulation—but it is something that you should be well aware of.

The idea here is that some people are simply contrarian: When they are told not to do something, they feel that deep desire to do it anyway. They find that they really want to do it instead of giving in to it. They want to find a way for themselves to avoid doing what they were told what to do. Because of this, if you know that someone is likely to respond like this, all you have to do is make it a point to understand the impulse. You simply tell them to do the opposite of what you want from them, and they, because of their contrarian nature, do the opposite. Of course, they do exactly what you want when you encourage this, and you get your way after all. However, not everyone is going to fit into this. You will need to be mindful of how you utilize this.

Reverse psychology is one of those things that work in many ways that might sound like they do not make much sense at first but are actually highly effective. If you want to make sure that you are getting that reaction from people that you want, you will need to ensure that you also understand what they do and when they do it. You must make sure that you figure out what you want from them, and what the opposite of this is as well.

Using Reverse Psychology

If you want to use reverse psychology, you need to make sure that you approach the person the right way. First, are they someone that is going to respond to reverse psychology? Not everyone will—it takes a certain kind of contrarian to give in to reverse psychology so you can utilize it yourself. It takes a certain kind of contrarian for you to ensure that everyone around you is going to behave a certain way when you suggest something. Thankfully, there are some tips and tricks that can help you to tap into this use of reverse psychology for those who either hate being bossed around or for the overconfident people who believe that they have nothing to worry about.

Challenge the other person
First, you could consider challenging the other person to do something when you want the opposite. Challenge them while insisting that they cannot do what you want from them. You could tell them that there is no way that they can successfully do what you want from them. Or, you could tell them that they have no hope of getting what you want. This will then trigger them to feel compelled to prove you wrong. Their drive to prove you wrong will be enough for you to get that result that you were looking for.

Remain calm
Of course, when you are using reverse psychology, you should also remain calm at all times. This is necessary, so they feel like they are spiraling out of control. If you can encourage this the right way, you can get that success that you were looking for. The more that you do this, the more likely that you are to get that success the right way. This is especially important if you use reverse psychology on children—they need that stability and that calm attitude from you to show them that they can trust what is happening or that they are comfortable.

Make them think they chose it
The key goal here is to lead them to the action that you want while also making them think that they brought themselves there willingly. That is the real key here—those who fall for reverse psychology are those that are much less likely to fall for it otherwise if they do not wholeheartedly believe that they chose out what they are doing or how they are doing it. This means that you must find a way to make it their own idea before they insist on anything else.

Remember your goal
As you use this form of influence on the other person, make sure that you do not lose sight of your real goal. Make sure that you cling to that idea of success and what it will be. You must ensure that you are on the right

page and that you continue to work toward what you wanted. This is imperative: You want to ensure that you can get it met, after all.

Say the opposite of what you want

When you utilize reverse psychology, everything is the opposite of what you want. You must make it clear to them that you want something that is contrary to what you actually want because that is what will trigger them to rebel- than getting you exactly what you wanted in the first place. You want to do this in an even tone. Do not let them think that you are lying, or they are going to see right through your attempts to control them in this way.

CHAPTER 11
Brainwashing

A very specific form of manipulation is known as brainwashing. This is something that only happens in very specific situations and must be deliberate. The process of brainwashing is unorthodox and largely illegal—but it is something that is possible to do. Through brainwashing, you are able to effectively convince someone to take an entirely new perspective on the world. You are effectively convincing them that they are someone new, building them a brand new identity that you control and influence. This is effectively just thought reform—it can be seen in all sorts of different contexts.

First, it is important to note that the information that you see here in front of you comes from an understanding of an event that happened to several American prisoners that were held during the Korean War. They were kept in camps and then brainwashed into believing that they were using germ warfare and that they must pledge their allegiance to the idea of communism and Korea. During this time, these prisoners had their entire minds erased. They were told to forget and relinquish their past lives and become someone new.

This is a form of mind control that works to completely rewrite the thoughts of someone else through forcefully breaking them down into someone that you can control. It is designed to inflict harm and distress to the point that they relinquish their past lives and choose to be whatever it is that you want them to be out of self-preservation and as you go through the steps involved, you will see how this new persona is developed, created and crafted entirely by captors that want nothing more than to control the individual and make them who they want.

Brainwashing works because the person that does the brainwashing in the first place gets complete control over the target. The person that is brainwashed has no choice but to obey or be harmed. Over time, the brainwasher is then able to completely dismantle that personality, little by little, until the new one is crafted to the individual's liking. The one that was brainwashed then adopts that new personality in hopes of remaining safe long-term.

How Brainwashing Works

Brainwashing is something that takes place over ten distinct steps that come together and create that final instance in which people are stuck with whatever happens. It works through brutally dismantling everything that the individual knows, discarding those identities and allegiances until only the desired person is left behind for them.

Assault on identity

This first step is designed to create complete destruction of the self. It is meant to destroy one's identity, little by little. This is done by telling someone that everything they thought that they knew was false. There are common questions about one's identity here, and each time, they are then disregarded. Perhaps their name is asked, and they are told that they are wrong, or if they say they have family, they are told that is a lie. The context for this step is that the attacker must deny everything that the individual says about themselves. Everything is deemed to be false when they try to assert themselves, and as a result, they feel confused. This should happen in particular through to the point of exhaustion to be fully effective. When the individual is thoroughly exhausted or vulnerable, often through sleep deprivation and starvation to create that vulnerability, they will give in, and slowly, their own understanding of who they are as an individual is entirely dismantled.

Guilt

Next comes guilt. With this stage, the individual is made to feel guilty. They are told that everything is their fault, and the guilt is often tied specifically to their identity. By assigning guilt as a defining factor of who someone is, there is that additional control over them. It allows for that full claiming of who they are and what they do. It allows for the brainwasher to step in and assert that they must reject everything. The idea here is that an identity that is wrapped up in guilt is easier to give up than one wrapped in positivity.

Self-betrayal

The third is self-betrayal. This is the stage in which the agent, the one doing the brainwashing, is able to get the target to agree with the assertions and attempt to assign guilt. This is to cause the individual to recognize that they were bad so that they can let go of who they were before. They need to feel like their choices were wrong so that they can let them go.

Breaking point

The breaking point comes after the betrayal of the self. It is the point at which the individual gives up—they just cannot do it any longer. They may have a complete nervous breakdown at this stage, crying and depressed, or even feel like they must commit suicide or harm themselves.

Leniency

However, when everything seems lost, and hope is abandoned, the brainwasher steps in to offer just a smidge of kindness—a touch of leniency that is meant to help. At the moment, when everything is bleak, this tiny act of kindness becomes enough to allow for that brainwashing to work entirely. You will see that someone may give you a sip of water, or they might also make a move to change how they talk. They might offer a cigarette or a bit of extra food. This makes the individual feel like they are in debt.

Releasing guilt

After that point of kindness, the individual often feels a desire to confess to release the guilt that they have. They feel like there is hope—but to get that hope back, they must reject everything that they have clung to just a bit more. They must make sure that they are able to get what they want and to get it, they let go of everything. Their will to live makes them feel like the only way to stay safe is if they confess.

Channeling guilt
At this point, they assume that they were the problem all along. They assume that all problems were their own doing and that if they want them fixed, they will have to do something about it. They will need to channel that guilt so that they can begin to release it. Often, this is done by wrapping their guilt around their identity and then choosing to start rejecting it.

Progress toward harmony
Next comes the desire to begin moving toward salvation or the goodness that they think that they can get if they denounce who they were before. This progression toward harmony involves them choosing to let go of what they thought they were and accepting the ideas from their captors or brainwashers. They start to recognize that through compliance and assimilation, they can escape the abuse. To make this happen, they start complying with assimilation demands. They take on that reliable, new identity at the urging of their brainwashers.

Final confession
Finally, it all ends when the new life is adopted completely. All old beliefs are rejected, and instead, the individual pledges allegiance to that brand new life and identity. This usually involves some sort of ceremony that allows them to take on that identity in a crowd. At this point, they are recognized as being fully assimilated and are allowed to interact with other people, who may or may not accept them.

CHAPTER 12
Seduction

Have you ever wished that you could seduce someone else? It is something that some people wish that they could do on a whim—maybe they see someone that they are attracted to. Perhaps they feel like they must do it if they want to be in a relationship. Maybe they just want a one-night-stand. No matter what, however, seduction is something that can be mastered relatively easily. If you know what you are doing and you are ruthless enough to not care about this idea of trying to get someone to want you, then you can utilize seduction with ease. You just have to know what you are getting yourself into.

This is a skill that is perfect if it is not yet time to settle down, but you could really use a night or two of some fun with someone new. If someone catches your eye at the bar, you might want to try to win them over, and the easiest way to do so is through seduction. If you feel like you really want someone to want you, you need to trigger it if it is not an instantaneous occurrence. Most of the time, attraction happens almost immediately, so if you do not notice it right off the bat when you get started in an interaction, then you might want to find a way to make it happen otherwise.

First of all, let's identify the fact that anyone can seduce someone else—male or female; you are capable of influencing someone in this manner if you know what you are doing. If you know how to talk to them or what they might want, you can encourage them to feel like they must actually want you after all. You just have to tap into those feelings and make them happen for yourself. If you can do that, you will be successful here.

In this chapter, we have a few key points to address. First, we will take some time to work out a proper definition of seduction. Then, we will look at how you can choose the right target. After all, not all people can be swayed in the same ways, and if you do not know what you are doing, you might pick out the wrong person—which could very quickly backfire. Then, you must figure out what it is that you can do to begin to seduce other people. By working through all three of these topics, you should be prepared to use it if you choose to do so.

What Is Seduction?

Before we begin, let's touch upon the idea of seduction. Though it is commonly believed to be morally corrupt or the act of leading someone astray, it is not exactly just that. It is a bit more. Though contextually, it sounds like you are simply trying to hurt someone with how you engage with them, there is more to it. It is not inherently corruptive, though it absolutely can be if you choose to target someone that is already in a relationship.

What it is, however, is a way to sway someone to do something that they may not have thought they would do initially. You could seduce someone into being attracted to you. It could be getting someone else to want to pursue you. It could also be attempting to convince them to go on a date with you. However, keep in mind that there is a difference between seduction, which is encouraging them to consent to do what you want, and forcing your will upon someone else. Seduction is a way in which you pursue someone else into making them consent without trying to coerce them. It is important to remember that your seduction should not go past that idea of consent and if you get a clear and resounding no, then you must respect that.

Choosing a Target

Seduction is a bit tricky to manage—the most important step of all is making sure that the person that you are trying to seduce is a proper target. You must make sure that you are choosing someone that is open to your advances, or at the very least, is not entirely shut down by them. You want to make sure that they are going to be willing. They need to *want* to be seduced. If they do not seem like they are very willing or receptive, there is probably a reason for it, and you should not attempt to coerce them into it. Remember, coercion is not seduction—you must mind the line to avoid falling into that trap. You need to bear in mind that seduction is something more nuanced.

To be open for seduction, consider three key points: Receptiveness, unhappiness, and alluring or attractiveness. Your idea target will hit all three of these points—they will be interested in being seduced for one reason or another, and this often overlaps with that unhappiness that comes with a desire for more. When you see this, you usually find someone at the end of a relationship or wishing that they were able to get out of the relationship and find someone new. There is something about their current relationship that is inherently unsatisfying, and when you show up, you represent that ability to get more. Finally, they must be attractive to you somehow, so you actually feel like you want to pursue them.

If your target does not fit all three of these points, then someone is going to end up unhappy. Now, you might enjoy the thrill of the chase in pursuing someone, but if you are not actually attracted to them, you are not going to be very happy with the end result either way. You are not going to want to be with them if you do not like them or find that you are entirely turned off by them. Because of this, you must consider all points. Once you do that, you can start seducing.

Using Seduction

When it comes to seducing, there are all sorts of different techniques that you can use based upon the target that you have chosen and just how receptive or not receptive that you think that they will be. How likely do you think that they are to want to do something? Let's go over several seductive strategies—you can choose out the ones that work the best for you. Remember, this is a sort of trial and error situation—it will take time and effort to figure out what works well for different people, and with every new target that you seduce, you will see that there are very different results that you can get.

Mixed signals

When you send mixed signals to someone else, you are effectively attempting to make yourself stand out or be memorable. You are essentially working to make yourself interesting—you send these mixed signals that make you paradoxical, which is inherently intriguing just by virtue of being a paradox. You will naturally get people's attention when you appear to be two contradictory things. You will be exciting, and that draws people into you. Through making it a point to show several different kinds of qualities, some of which may be quite contradictory, you start to get attention directed right toward yourself.

In doing this, you make yourself seem interesting one way or another. Think about the person that you are targeting and figure out what you think they would like. Are they talking to all of the "bad boys" at the bar? Make yourself seem tougher, but then just as quickly, also show a tender side. Maybe someone drops something, and you stop to give it to them, or you offer your prime seat at the bar to an older gentleman who came in to watch the game. By doing something that is sympathetic and kind, you display that you are not all bad and show them that they can, and they will be able to expect you to be kinder in many different situations. This works well and shows depth in your personality as well—something that many people often forget all about.

Make yourself desirable

You should also work to make sure that you come across as desirable as well. Remember that principle of scarcity? Time to make use of it—it is time to appeal to the idea that you look like you are scarce by getting the attention of other people. By making the individual that you are interested in believe that you are in demand with other people, you are much more likely to get them to come toward you quickly. They will want to ensure that they are getting those results that they are looking for. Overall, if other people find you fascinating or interesting, you must be worthy, and people will start to flock to you as well.

Make the other person feel anxious

Remember, one of the best things that you can play up during this whole process is anxiety. This is important—you want to remind the other person of just how unhappy they are, so they start to see you as an option to finding the solution to the unhappiness that you have in the first place. The more that you do this, the more likely that you are to get that unhappiness all settled and resolved. You effectively want them to feel anxious in covert ways. You want them to be unaware of what is happening so you can actually make it work for you in the first place. You want to do this all as covertly as possible as well—you don't want them to be aware of what you are doing or how you are actively attempting to pursue them.

Adapt to their preferences
If you are trying to seduce someone, then you must become whatever it is that they want from you. If they want you to be someone that is going to be kinder, then do that. If they seem to want those tough guys, then be that as well. You want to work to create an artificial image of yourself in the other person's mind effectively. You want them to feel like they want you at all costs. You want them to feel like you are highly desirable or like they will not get you if they do not know what they are doing. By making sure that you show them what they want to see, you can actually win them over quicker.

Lay on the sweet talk
People do not listen very well when they do not hear what they want to hear. This means that if you want someone's attention, you want to tell them what they do want to hear. The more that you can do that, the more likely that you are to actually get them to look to you. They will see that you are saying what they want to hear, and they will then pay closer attention. Why wouldn't they? Sweet talk them—inflate their egos a bit. Make them feel good, so they like you more. This will help you to win them over and get that result that you want. You will trigger them to feel compelled to follow along with what you want.

Tempt them
When you tempt them, you will show them what they could have instead of what they currently do. You are showing them that a slight glimpse through the fence that shows them that the grass is greener—but by doing so in the way that you do, you are making them want to follow you. Let them see a bit of what things could be like if they chose you. Maybe flirt with them. Build that sexual tension. Create that spark of attraction and chemistry that is undeniable for them—they will want to pursue it. That little glimpse can become all-consuming and drive them to want to be around you more. If you play your cards just right, you will be able to get them to want you.

Parent your target
This might seem somewhat counterintuitive but consider for a moment that for most people, they felt the safest as a child when they were with their parents. People look back fondly to their childhoods when they were sheltered, safe, and free to do what they wanted when they wanted it, and because of that, you can actually start to trigger those happy feelings and those fond moments of being taken care of just by being careful around the person that you want to attract. If you know what you are doing, you can start to care for them, little by little. Suggest that they put on a jacket because it is cold. Offer to get something for them. Keep them safe. By

being concerned for their wellbeing, you can make them feel more secure with you, and that will also trigger them to be more interested in you as well.

Make insinuations

When you insinuate something, you say something without having to say the words, implying it through indirect language that you use to seduce them. You are trying to create that degree of uncertainty that will help you to take control of the situation that you are in to properly lead the other person. If you know what you are doing, you can get them to want to follow you and what you are doing and saying.

Create suspense

By creating a suspenseful feeling, you will effectively encourage them to become interested in you. Because they cannot tell what will come next or what you will do, you become interesting to them. They decide that they want to pursue you just because they are unsure of what to expect, and they do not know how to deal with the situation or what they should be doing. By carefully fabricating situations in which the suspense can be maintained, you can keep your target interested in you for far longer than you probably realized you could. This is perfect for you if you are unsure of what you will be doing long-term in that relationship.

Play the victim

Though it can seem counterintuitive, playing the victim will actually help you immensely here—it will help you to properly recognize that point in which you are in control of a situation. When you play the victim the right way, you can follow that line between showing that you are manipulating so much that they can see it right in front of them and being too light on trying to influence them. You want to make it so that they think they are superior, and you are the one that is vulnerable. By making yourself the vulnerable one, you make it so that they believe that you are not a threat. This will grant you that power to seduce them longer term.

Balance the highs and lows

Another point to consider is making sure that you are not too nice. You need to balance out the highs and the lows to maintain that type of appearance that you want. Kindness and niceness are great in a relationship, but if you are just seducing someone, you need to recognize that they are also boring because they are safer. You want to make sure that you are not making yourself boring—instead, work to ensure that you appear to be interesting. Make lows that make the high points in your relationship or interactions seem better. Consider this for a moment: In a relationship, if the neutral state is you simply getting along and aiming to please, it can be quite boring to be there with someone else. However, when you add in those artificial lows, the neutral and high points of your interactions become that much more compelling for you instead. Make them feel guilty sometimes or insecure sometimes so that when you make them feel special, it is even more special than it would have been.

CHAPTER 13
Spotting Manipulation

Finally, the last chapter in this book is all about figuring out where the manipulation lies. Though you now know how to influence people in many different ways, it is time to recognize that there is more to it than meets the eye. When you want to manipulate someone else, you must make it a point to understand their own vulnerabilities, but what about your own? When it comes to being able to navigate through the world, you must also be able to spot manipulation so that you can control it yourself as well. You must be able to protect yourself from the manipulative attempts all around you—you need to find ways that you can spot it before it ever becomes a problem for you.

Thankfully, or not so thankfully, manipulation is something that is relatively easy to spot if you know what you are looking for and if you can keep your attention where it needs to be. By learning the signs of manipulation, you can spot it before it happens to you. Remember, manipulation can happen in just about any context. It could occur in a relationship, in a family situation, or otherwise. It could happen at work, or it could be something that only happens with a certain friend. No matter when or where it happens, it is important to note that being manipulated is not fun. It is not typically a good feeling to realize that other people have been trying to control you, and you will want to try to do something to prevent it, if at all possible. If you are trying to spot manipulation in your own life, try to keep an eye out for these various signs that we are going to be going over—they will help you to spot when there is a problem or if you need to do something else to prevent it.

Constant Accusations

When someone is manipulating you, they will constantly accuse you of things. They will make you feel like you are being controlled or like you have to give in to them. Their accusations leave you wondering what is going on and leave you feeling entirely trapped in the situation that you are in. They may accuse you of lying or cheating even when you are not, and they actually are. This is a common projection method that will happen.

Additionally, you might feel like you have to accuse the manipulator as well because not everything seems quite right. You cannot put your finger on it, but things are going wrong, and you blame them for it—something that they then vehemently deny. They do not take fault at all.

Mind Games

Mind games happen regularly when you are in the presence of a manipulator. Just consider the context of this entire book—much of it involved playing mind games to control the other party. If you feel like you are constantly being controlled, it is time to consider that the relationship that you have with the individual is actually manipulative. Keep in mind, however, that they will not concede defeat. They will not admit when they are at fault because they want to keep you easy to control and docile, and that is often done through sheer instability. They want you to feel like you are unstable so they can maintain control over the situation.

Your Items Keep Getting Damaged

If you find that your objects are constantly getting damaged, usually much more often than the other person's objects, then there is a chance that there is actually something more going on here. Often, manipulators will damage things that will cause feelings of distress or upset solely because they want that control. Remember, negative emotions are one of the biggest weaknesses that you can get from someone. This is meant to make you upset so you can be controlled more.

The Other Party Is Jealous

Jealousy often happens in the relationship, and often, the manipulator will also attempt to get it installed in the relationship to take control as well. They want you to feel like you are jealous so they can wield that jealousy as a tool for themselves. If you voice a complaint, they will simply say that you are jealous and that they can do what they want. Think about how a manipulator might flirt with someone in front of their partner and, when confronted, say that the other party was simply too jealous and that they should not have been so concerned.

The Other Party Is Always a Victim

If you notice that the other party is always a victim when you are in a relationship, this is often an attempt to influence or manipulate the other party. It is done for that degree of control and is entirely intentional. By being the victim, the individual can then trigger guilt in you so that you feel much more likely to give them what they want. They want you to feel guilty so that they can avoid the blame while still maintaining that control over the situation. If you want to avoid being manipulated, then you must make sure that you spot the victims and weed them out of your life.

You Are Rushed Into Choices

If you feel like you are constantly being rushed into decisions, whether you should be or not, there is a real chance that you are being manipulated. This is done, so you do not have the time to think things through. If you had that time to think, then you might make a rational choice that would not represent what the manipulator wants. Instead, they decide to make the choices for you. They choose to push you to choose quickly, so they get to keep that control longer-term.

There Are Inconsistencies

If your entire relationship is defined by constant inconsistencies in actions and words, it is quite possibly manipulative. Manipulators are experts at saying things that they know the other party wants to hear solely because they want the other party to give in to them. They want to get the other party to do whatever they want, so they tell them something, only to renege on it later. This is common—they are betting on your complacency after you agree to do something, and they do not want to deal with it. If you know what you are doing, however, you can prevent this from becoming too problematic for yourself. You can stop the inconsistencies when you realize that they are there.

Everything Is a Negotiation

If everything that you do in your relationship is fraught with negotiation, there is a good chance that you are being manipulated into doing things for the other person. This is there to allow for the manipulator to get what they want while making the other party feel like they have a say when they really did not. They will make sure that they come out on top every single time while also making the victim feel like they gained something in the entire situation, even if there was nothing to gain in the first place.

Words Are Distorted

If you notice that what you say is constantly being taken out of context, then you are being manipulated. The best manipulators are able to take what someone said and spin it around so that the meaning they spin is the opposite of what was intended. This is done so they can then emotionally blackmail the other party into admitting their faults so they can take and maintain control over the situation. Through doing this little by little, they can ensure that they get to take over everything without much of a problem or battle.

You Constantly Feel Upset Around One Person

If you notice that you are only upset when you are around one person, or if your emotions are always frazzled after interactions with just one person, there is probably a good reason for that and that good reason is probably that you are being influenced in some significant way that you should consider fixing. If you constantly find yourself upset, look at the person that is causing those feelings. Why do they trigger them? If you really think about it, they are probably manipulating you.

You Feel a Strong Sense of Obligation for Someone

Likewise, if you feel an unnaturally strong sense of obligation toward someone that you cannot really explain, there is a good chance that you feel that due to some degree of manipulation that you will need to offset. If you know what you are doing, you should be able to prevent it. Spot the reason for the obligation. It is likely to be manipulative in nature, and when you spot it, you can then prevent it from controlling you.

You Feel Like You Have Changed
Finally, if you feel like you have changed more than makes sense considering the situation that you are in, it is time for you to start piecing together why. Figure out what it is that is causing these problems. Figure out why it is that you feel the way that you do, then make sure that you can influence or control it. Make sure that you figure out what you can do to stop it. Usually, that means that you will have to cut off the manipulator so you can protect yourself.

CONCLUSION

Thank you for making it through to the end of *Manipulation Techniques*. Let's hope it was informative and able to provide you with all of the tools you need to achieve your goals, whatever they may be.

At this point, you understand now what it is to influence other people. You have discovered the art of being able to directly influence and take charge of people so that you can assert what you want when you want it. You have now seen several different methods that you can use to influence other people, and because of that, you have now discovered what it will take for you to maintain that control long term. If you want to make sure that you can control those people around you, you will need to put these different tools to the test so that you can take charge where you need it. Remember, you now have all the power—all the cards in your hands.

As you read through this book, you were guided through several key ways that you could start to change the way that people acted, and it all began with a thought. It all began with being able to change that one individual thought so you could watch the feelings and behaviors follow along. By changing one thought, you can create an entirely different feeling. By changing one feeling, you can create a dramatically different behavior from what you may have initially expected. Because of this, you want to consider the different ways that people engage with each other. You want to consider that ultimately, we all behave differently. We all engage differently. We all act differently, and it all starts with the thought.

From here, it is time for you to decide what you will do with your newfound knowledge. Are you going to make use of it for yourself? Are you going to influence yourself and how you engage with people? Are you going to control other people instead? Are you going to make sure that you come out on top, no matter what happens next? No matter where you decide that you are going next, one thing is for sure: You have the power. You can choose where it will be.

Remember, your power is one that you must use responsibly. You must choose how you wish to proceed now that you have this information for yourself. If you choose to use it for your own benefit, then you must also be ready to take responsibility for the actions as well. If the results are worth it to you, then what you do is your own choice. Remember to keep that in mind and also recognize how your actions will influence those around you at the same time. Make sure that you take the time to really recognize the ways that people around you engage. Take the time to consider how different people will interact with each other. Make sure that you are confident about your behaviors. Not all manipulation or influence is inherently bad—it has its own place sometimes, and sometimes it makes perfect sense to use it. However, that is something that you must work out over time. That is something for you to figure out on your own terms.

Nevertheless, you now have the information that you will need. Thank you for taking the time to read through this book. Thank you for considering everything that you know now about manipulation. Hopefully, you are ready to take the information out with you into the world to do the best possible things that you can do, and hopefully, as you do navigate, you make good choices.

Now, it is time for you to head out into the world and make use of this information. Hopefully, you feel a bit better with it in mind so you can use it if necessary. And finally, please consider taking the time to leave a review if you found that the information that you read in this book was useful. If it benefitted you, please let us know how. Your feedback is something that is always greatly appreciated and provides plenty to help ensure that future books work just as well as this one! And, if there are any suggestions that you have or if there is anything that you wish this book had covered, please consider leaving that behind in your review as well. Any feedback that you provide will make the next book even better than this one!

Thank you once more, and good luck out there with this information! Hopefully, you are able to succeed in everything that you set out to do and more!

DESCRIPTION

Are you interested in being able to manipulate others? Have you wondered what you could do if you wanted to control the other people in your life? If so, then keep reading... This book could be exactly what you are looking for. When it comes to being able to influence and control the minds of other people, you want to ensure that you know what you are doing.

Remember, not all manipulation is bad. Manipulation is simply to mold someone—to make them do something through the power of your own influence. When you influence someone else through manipulation, you covertly pull strings to get them to do whatever it is that you needed from them. You can frame something a certain way, or you behave a certain way as well. You could choose to talk to someone to convince them to change up their thought processes, or you could persuade them to take your side by utilizing the principles of persuasion. One thing is for sure; however—there are many, many different options that you can use to make people believe whatever it is that you want.

Through developing the right way to approach the situation, you can put yourself in that position to help yourself. If you wanted to do so, you could make it happen yourself. When you read through this book, you will learn precisely how to influence and control the people around you. As you develop this skill, you develop the ability that you will need to keep in mind if you want to control other people. From emotional manipulation to persuasion and brainwashing or mind control, you can develop the ability to learn these different skills so you can be successful at influencing other people. You can expect to see:

- An understanding of what manipulation is and how it works
- Why the subconscious mind is key in using these techniques
- How you can begin to manipulate others
- Using emotional manipulation on other people to get them to do what you want when you want it
- Using mind control on other people and how it works
- Using NLP on other people, as well as several different methods that you can use
- Discovering the power of body language and how it can influence other people with just simple changes to how you stand about
- Developing the ability to utilize the principles of persuasion to control other people with your words, convincing them to trust your judgment
- Learning how to hypnotize people with ease so you can speak directly to their subconscious minds

- Discovering the power of reverse psychology and when and how it works
- Working on how to brainwash other people and how it works
- Developing the ability to use seduction
- Learning how to spot manipulation before it happens to you
- *AND MORE*

As you read through this book, you can learn everything you will need to know to control other people and how you can protect yourself as well. If you are ready to take control so you can be in charge, then you are in the right place—let's get started to see what you need to do. All you have to do is scroll up and click on BUY NOW today to get started!

www.ingramcontent.com/pod-product-compliance
Lightning Source LLC
Chambersburg PA
CBHW071510070526
44578CB00001B/500